A Manuscript Index to the *Index of Middle English Verse*

RICHARD HAMER

THE BRITISH LIBRARY

This *Manuscript Index to the Index of Middle English Verse* is published in association with the series *English Manuscript Studies 1100–1700*, edited by Peter Beal and Jeremy Griffiths, in which the *Index* was originally to have appeared. The British Library is grateful to the editors for allowing the *Index* to be issued as a separate publication.

First published 1995 by
The British Library
Great Russell Street, London WC1B 3DG
British Library Cataloguing in Publication Data
A cataloguing record for this title is available
from The British Library

ISBN 0-7123-0387-1

Designed by John Mitchell
Typeset by Bexhill Phototypesetters, Bexhill-on-Sea
Printed in England by
Henry Ling Printers Ltd, Dorchester

Contents

Preface

The *Index of Middle English Verse* (1947) by Carleton Brown and Russell Hope Robbins with its Supplement (1965) by Robbins and John C. Cutler (hereafter *IMEV* and *SUP*) remains an indispensable aid to Middle English studies; but its compilers did not supply an index to the manuscripts cited. This is an attempt to fill the gap.

In this index each manuscript is listed under its present location, and followed by the *IMEV* numbers of its citations. Where these were corrected or superseded in the Supplement they are given only in the final form. Additional copies of the items and recently discovered verses have not been added (though notes have been kept of any which have come to my attention); but manuscripts known to have moved or whose locations have been newly identified are cross-referenced to their former designations, and wrong or incomplete entries have been corrected.

As far as practicable entries have been checked, though sometimes this has been limited to confirming with a published catalogue that the citation is at least feasible; but in doubtful cases further checks have been made by visiting or by consulting the librarians concerned. Where a reference system has been changed since *IMEV* and *SUP* were published, both forms are given. On the whole Arabic numerals are used instead of Roman.

After the main index there are three smaller ones listing printed books containing ME verses (as handwritten marginalia or the like), epitaphs and inscriptions (the continued existence of these has not been verified), and missing or unidentified manuscripts. The compiler or the editors of *English Manuscript Studies 1100–1700* would be grateful to receive any corrections to the indexes or identifications of the missing ones so that from time to time such information can be published.

To acknowledge properly the generous help received in identifying and locating manuscripts I should have to list the librarians and archivists of most of the institutions named and many other individuals. My special thanks are due to Dr A. I. Doyle, Dr A. S. G.

Edwards, Mr Jeremy Griffiths, Dr Christopher de Hamel, Dr Margaret Laing, Mr Richard Linenthal and Miss J. C. Ringrose. Among many catalogues and other published works used I am especially indebted to Robert E.Lewis and Angus McIntosh, *A descriptive guide to the manuscripts of the Prick of Conscience*, Julia Boffey, *Manuscripts of English courtly love lyrics*, and Siegfried Wenzel, *Preachers, poets and the early English lyric*. My thanks also go to Mr Anthony Martin, formerly of the Middle English Dialect Project at Edinburgh University, whose idea this index was and who put much of the basic information onto a database; Professor Michael Benskin, who drew my attention to this work and persuaded me to take it on; and Mr L. D. Burnard and Ms B. Crutch of the Oxford University Computing Service, who have devised the means of manipulating the material on the computer.

Richard Hamer

List of Abbreviations

Kane A-Text	Kane, George, ed., *Piers Plowman: the A version*, London, 1960.
Ker Pastedowns	Ker, N. R., '*Pastedowns in Oxford Bindings*', Oxford Bibliographical Society, new series V, Oxford, 1954.
Lewis & McIntosh	Lewis, R. E., and McIntosh, A., *A descriptive guide to the manuscripts of the Prick of Conscience*, Medium Ævum Monographs, new series XII, Oxford, 1982.
MMBL	Ker, N. R. and Piper, A. J., *Medieval Manuscripts in British Libraries*, 4 vols, Oxford, 1969–92.
Ricci	Ricci, Seymour de, *Census of Medieval and Renaissance Manuscripts in the United States and Canada*, 3 vols. and supplement, New York, 1935–62.
Riverside Chaucer	Benson, Larry D., *The Riverside Chaucer*, 3rd edn., Boston, U.S.A., 1987.

Index of Manuscripts

Aberdeen, City Archives
Minute Book of Seisins ii (iii in *SUP*):
912.5/1, 2821.3/3
Minute Book of Seisins iii: 470.5/2

Aberdeen, Univ. Lib.
21: 399.5/6, 746.5/6, 1426.6/6,
1637.6/6, 2361.5/6, 2736.2/6, 2831.4/6,
3218.3/6, 4189.5/6
123: 2153.5/1, 3694.3/2
154: 3902/2, 4038/2, 4129/5, 4273.5/1
223: 1338.5/1

Aberystwyth, National Lib. of Wales
733B: 1459/A13, 1459/B16
734B (no number in *IMEV*): 595/19
5043: 2837/5, 2916/4, 3030/4, 3037/18
21972D (Merthyr fragment): 4019/59
Add.441C: 4008/A6
Llanstephan 119: 4008/A7, 4008/C17
Mostyn Welsh 129: 474/1, 952/3,
3571/2
Peniarth 22: 2698/12
Peniarth 26: 23.5/1, 152/1, 552.3/1,
366.5/1, 3306.5/1, 4008/A3, 4008/Ad,
4008/C15, 4018.5/1, 4029/12
Peniarth 50: 949/1, 1153.5/1, 1564/1,
3091.5/1, 4008/A4, 4029/13, 4038.5/1
Peniarth 53: 33.3/1, 1726/1, 1727/19
Peniarth 58: 4029/14
Peniarth 92: 4113/17
Peniarth 94: 4008/A5, 4008/C16
Peniarth 98: 2514/2
Peniarth 111: 2514/3
Peniarth 114: 1381/1
Peniarth 196: 2514/4
Peniarth 356: 69.5/1, 342.5/1, 513/6,
793.5/1, 1941.5/1, 3274/3, 3324/1,
3439.5/1, 3502.5/3, 4034.3/1, 4128.4/1
Peniarth 393: 4019/45
Peniarth 394: 77/6, 83/2
Peniarth 395: 245/32, 2320/C9,
4121/1, 4268/3
Peniarth 399: 716/11
Peniarth 481: 854/28, 3955/18

Porkington 10: 4/1, 22/3, 298/1,
324/10, 341/1, 349/3, 369/1, 479/1,
559/2, 560/3, 674/10, 704/15, 977/5,
1116/2, 1120/1, 1241/1, 1641/9, 1785/2,
1852/1, 1888/2, 1897/3, 1932/1, 1957/2,
2018/1, 2610/1, 3289/9, 3314/1, 3330/1,
3363/1, 3743/2, 4001/1, 4029/17
Porkington 20: 1961/11, 3184/4,
3428/80

**Aldenham, Goldschmidt Cat.55 item 59,
now Cleveland, Ohio,
W.90.91.92.C.468**

**Allan of Darlington, now British Lib.
Egerton 2810**

**Alnwick Castle, Duke of
Northumberland**
455: 3926/1 (55 in *IMEV*), 4019/49
D.XI.1: 2698/14, 4113/19 (D.X.1 in
IMEV)

Antwerp, Plantin-Moretus Museum
57 (M 305): 1392.5/1

**Appleby Castle, Lord Hothfield (not
Hotham), on deposit at Yorks
Archaeological Society, Leeds**:
595/21

Armagh, Diocesan Registry
Bp.John Swayne's Register: 811/2

Arras, Bibl. de la Ville
184 (254): 2289.3/1, 2607/3

Arundel Castle, Duke of Norfolk
Arundel-Harington MS: 232/4,
3361.1/1, 3361.6/2
Prick of Conscience: 3428/95

**Ashburnham App.243, now Manchester,
Rylands Eng.90**

Asloan, Mrs John McCombe: 54/1,
276.5/3, 303.3/1, 417.5/2, 636/1,
1082.5/1, 1119.3/2, 1507/8, 1554/2,

(continued overleaf)

Asloan, Mrs John McCombe
2289.8/3, 2461/2, 2831.8/3, 3187/D1, 3442/2, 3584/3, 3703/4

Austin, Univ. of Texas
8: 3448/1
143 (olim Brudenell, Sotheby Feb 1959): 2784/11, 3928/21, 4019/46

Basel, Univ. Lib.
B.VIII.4: 63.5/1, 442/2, 591.5/1, 3389.8/1

Beeleigh Abbey, Christina Foyle
Mirror of Man's Salvacioun (olim Huth): 1511.5/1
Prick of Conscience: 3428/74
Rolle's Form of Living (olim Harmsworth): 2017.5/26, 4056/25
Speculum Christiani: 1342/38, 2119/53, 2167/45, 3687/18, 4150/33

Belfast, Queen's Univ.
3/11B (no number in *IMEV*): 3491/7

Belvoir Castle, Duke of Rutland
Fall of Princes: 1168/20

Berkeley, Univ. of California
75 (olim John Gribbel, Philadelphia): 1168/27

Berlin, Staatsbibl.
Theol.lat.fol 249: 1631.3/1, 2794.6/1, 3167.3/1, 3897.5/1, 3900.5/1

Blackburn, Museum & Art Gallery
091.21040 (no number in *IMEV*): 2672/5

Blairs College (deposited at National Lib. of Scotland)
13 (=*MMBL* 9): 1370/7, 2577/10, 3305.8/2
22 (=*MMBL* 1): 914/4
Book of Hours (=*MMBL* 6): 2119/52

Boston, Mass., Medical Lib.
23: 1999/1

Boston, Mass., Public Lib.
1519 (=Ricci 92): 2784/12, 3491/16
1521 (=Ricci 94): 3928/31
1527(=Ricci 100) (from Kraus Cat.22 no. 21): 3694.3/4 = also 3694.3/5
1546 (=Ricci 124) (olim Sowter): 605.5/1, 624/13, 3238.3/1
f.med.94 (olim Campbell, Robinson Cat.74 1944, no. 268): 3928/30

Brechin Castle, Earl of Dalhousie
Fordun's Chronicle, at SRO, GD5/26/48: 1181/2
Wintoun's Chronicle: 399/5A

Bridgewater, Corporation Muniments
123, now Taunton, Somerset RO, D/B/bw 123

Bristol, All Saints Church
2: 3559.5/1

Bristol, Avon County Lib.
10 (no number in *IMEV*): 2516/15

Brough Hall
Psalter, now Oxford, Bodleian, lat.liturg.g.8
York Manual, now Cambridge, Mass., Harvard, Widener Lib. 1

Brudenell
Sotheby Feb 1959, now Austin, Texas 143
Sydrac fragment, now Northants RO, Bru.I.v.101

Brussels, Bibl. Royale
2054: 2118/6, 3905.5/1
4628: 3430/3
not identified: 3883/6

Buccleuch, Quaritch Cat.304, now San Marino, Huntington HM 131

Buckland House, see Coughton Court

Buhler, see New York, Pierpont Morgan, series B

Bute, Marquess of
Northern Homily Cycle, now Cambridge Univ. Lib. Add.8335
Confessio Amantis, now privately owned: 2662/A23

Cambridge, Clare College
5: 4104/1
13: 49/1

Cambridge, Corpus Christi College
8: 1500.5/1, 4221/1
26: 2988/5
59: 2815/1
61: 1955.5/1, 3327/6
78: 4181/5
80: 842.5/1, 2312/1
145: 50/4, 56/4, 57/4, 58/4, 59/4, 82/7, 127/2, 721/7, 791/8, 907/4, 1788/4, 1809/6, 1859/8, 1911/8, 2127/5, 2304/7, 2755/6, 2839/9, 2842/7, 2843/7, 2844/8, 2845/4, 2850/9, 2854/10, 2856/7, 2858/7, 2860/8, 2866/10, 2868/8, 2872/7, 2874/7, 2876/7, 2878/8, 2880/10, 2882/6, 2884/10, 2889/8, 2895/6, 2905/10, 2906/6, 2910/10, 2911/2, 2912/7, 2918/8, 2922/6, 2932/11, 2945/8, 2949/9, 2950/10, 2951/8, 2956/6, 2957/8, 2960/5, 2973/5, 2987/8, 2989/9, 2990/9, 2991/7, 2994/7, 3004/9, 3017/6, 3026/9, 3029/A15,

3035/8, 3036/7, 3037/9, 3041/8, 3042/7, 3046/7, 3048/10, 3051/7, 3052/8, 3055/7, 3059/9, 3060/6, 3063/8, 3064/14, 3066/8, 3067/10, 3068/10, 3266/5, 3384/5, 3388/7, 3389/9, 3813/8, 4266/9
150: 3515.5/1
171: 4247/1
174: 4269.5/1
233: 88/1
278: 3103/3
293: 1459/C9
294: 268/1
298: 2601/1
301: 2698/6, 4113/9
313: 676/1
327: 2194/1
329: 3220.9/1
337: 4142/1
369: 3260/2
379: 3818/1
392: 2835/1
402: 3568/3
405: 228.8/1, 1047/1, 2641/1
417: 2296/1
423: 3687/15
441: 3513/1
444: 2072/1
496: 2229/14

Cambridge, Emmanuel College
27: 177/1, 580/1, 695/2, 1062/2, 1129/2 (not in fact present), 1545/1, 1599/1, 2137/1, 2187/1, 2291/1, 2694/1, 2704/1, 2769/1, 3100/1, 3884/1, 4227/1
106: 671/1, 2320/A7
246: 2776/1, 3499/7
263: 3318.4/2

Cambridge, Fitzwilliam Museum
55: 3585.5/1
56: 2493/2
261: 824/45
276*: 1364.5/4
355(a): 3236/4, 3943/14
40–1950: 914/10, 1727/15, 1786.5/1, 2154/2, 2388.5/1
41–1950 (40–1951 in *IMEV*): 914/9
McClean 123: 1272/4
McClean 128: 2304/10, 2850/12, 2861/2, 2870/6, 2873/7, 2875/11, 2880/13, 2886/9, 2889/11, 2896/4, 2912/10, 2961/10, 3005/9, 3033/11, 3037/12, 3059/12, 3063/11, 3068/13, 3813/11, 4266/12
McClean 130: 245/19
McClean 131: 3428/38
McClean 181: 1913/12, 4019/4
McClean 182: 447/4, 675/1, 935/7, 1168/9*, 2229/19, 3369/1, 3625/2, 4021/1
McClean 183: 935/8
McClean 184: 1597/12
McClean 185: 2229/20
Mu 1005 (formerly unnumbered fragment): 3193.5/1, 3724.5/2

Cambridge, Gonville and Caius College
54: 1121/1
71: 142/A6, 142/B7, 400/7, 498/7, 565/5, 594/5, 621/7, 798/6, 827.5/1, 1003/8, 1127/5, 1141/6, 1223/6, 1490/7, 1822/5, 1935/6, 2001/A5, 2001/B6, 2002/5, 2114/5, 2298/6, 2329/7, 2340/7, 2596/4, 2729/5, 2775/6, 2832/5, 3081/6, 3133/5, 3254/6, 3273/5, 3281/6, 3282/7, 3287/5, 3350/5, 3408/5, 3463/4, 3496/6, 3518/7, 3716/5, 3802/5, 3863/8, 4035/5, 4134/5, 4143/6, 4151/6
84: 3069/2, 3071/2, 3507/3
107: 3145/1
124: 233/4, 263/4, 1242/4, 1243/4, 1244/4, 1245/4, 1246/4, 1247/4, 1248/4, 1249/4, 1296/4, 1719/4, 2428/4
160: 245/16
168: 462/4, 4068.3/4
174: 604/1, 1480/1, 2413/2, 2714/3, 2780/5, 4246/5, 4249/2
175: 701/2, 1158/1, 1184/5, 1973/1, 1979/2, 1993/A2
176: 1827/1, 3787/3
201: 1459/B9
221: 1824/1, 2627.5/1, 3899.6/1
230: 858.5/1, 2574/12, 4184/4
249: 1824.6/1, 3632/16, 4029/3
261: 3209/1
334: 995.6/1, 3397/7
336: 935/20
351: 4110/1
364: 142/B8, 495/4, 565/6, 798/7, 827.5/2, 1003/9, 1150/6, 1204/6, 1321/4, 1822/6, 1935/7, 2001/A6, 2001/B7, 2002/6, 2058/5, 2077/5, 2114/6, 2298/7, 2329/8, 2596/5, 2775/7, 3081/7, 3147/5, 3273/6, 3275/6, 3281/7, 3282/8, 3287/6, 3339/6, 3408/6, 3463/5, 3802/6, 3863/9, 4143/7, 4151/7, 4239/5
365: 1820/2
383: 225/1, 236/2, 266.3/1, 521.5/1, 1280/1, 1330/1, 1849/1, 1892/2, 2109/1, 2185/1, 3174/1, 3971/1
386: 3428/32
394: 4063/1
399: 595/12
408: 4093/1
414: 1294.5/1
433: 1151/7
465: 4185.5/1
512: 1922/1

(continued overleaf)

Cambridge, Gonville and Caius College

513: 2605.5/1
609: 3694/1
669: 745/1, 2017.5/14, 4056/13
793: 576.5/1
804: 3844.8/1

Cambridge, Jesus College

13: 1307/1, 2074/1, 2117/1, 2240/1, 3210/1, 3937/1, 4185/2
22: 4167/1
51: 1342/14, 1491/9, 2119/12, 2167/15, 4150/12
56: 178/1, 401/4, 447/2, 448/2, 529/2, 824/12, 854/9, 1019/1, 1050/1, 1130/2, 1294/4, 1814/1, 1865/3, 2156/1, 2233/12, 2394/3, 2464/3, 2625/5, 2791/7, 2812/2, 3503/3, 3632/17, 3673/1, 3798/3, 3845/8, 4099/3, 4112/3, 4243/1, 4245/3
59: 2290.5/1
74: 905/1

Cambridge, King's College

13 I: 2843/8
13 II: 126/6, 273/5, 409/5, 443/7, 483/8, 578/4, 719/4, 791/9, 1546/7, 1809/7, 1859/9, 2106/5, 2120/6, 2647/7, 2755/7, 2844/9, 2854/11, 2884/11, 2905/11, 2989/10, 2990/10, 3281.5/1, 3664/6, 3766/5, 3767/5
Muniment Roll 2 W.32: 521/1

Cambridge, Magdalene College

5: 669/1, 1793/1, 4096/1
13: 940/1, 1051/1, 1502/4, 1679/1, 1937/1, 2689/1, 3087/5, 4129/3
18: 3428/33
19: 2631/1
Pepys 1036: 413.6/1, 4184/18
Pepys 1047: 189.5/1, 324/2, 854.8/1, 1197.2/1, 3254.5/1, 3255.5/1, 4187.5/1
Pepys 1236: 717/3, 1501/1, 2600/1, 2800/1, 3342/2, 3943/9, 3951.5/1
Pepys 1408 (no number in *IMEV*): 3138/1
Pepys 1461: 3491/3
Pepys 1576: 2497/1
Pepys 1584: 244/4, 257/2, 355/2, 1041/2, 1126/2, 1259/3, 1379/2, 1503/1, 1815/2, 1854/3, 2714/4, 2770/2, 3262/2, 3861/2, 4200/3
Pepys 1661: 2627/4
Pepys 1760: 1165/1
Pepys 2006: 100/A5, 239/6, 239/7, 809/8, 851/5, 854/10, 913/4, 991/3, 1168/5*, 1507/6, 3412/11, 3542/6, 3625/1, 3661/6, 3670/B, 3747/3, 3787/4, 3955/6, 4282/1
Pepys 2011: 2825/1, 3928/8
Pepys 2014: 727/B9, 1881/5
Pepys 2030: 1540/4, 1591/1
Pepys 2101: 2229/15
Pepys 2125: 197.8/4, 1128/1, 1194/1, 1259/4, 1367.5/4, 1409/1, 1761/4, 1825/1, 2250/5, 2270/5, 2725/1, 3397/2
Pepys 2163: 1934/3, 4174.5/1
Pepys 2344: 38/3, 50/5, 56/5, 57/5, 58/5, 59/5, 82/8, 126/7, 184/7, 201/7, 273/6, 276/3, 409/6, 443/8, 483/9, 578/5, 719/5, 721/8, 791/10, 907/5, 1546/8, 1788/5, 1809/8, 1859/10, 1911/9, 2105/4, 2106/6, 2120/7, 2127/6, 2304/8, 2632/3, 2647/8, 2755/8, 2839/10, 2842/8, 2843/9, 2844/10, 2845/5, 2848/7, 2850/10, 2854/12, 2856/8, 2858/8, 2860/9, 2866/11, 2868/9, 2870/4, 2872/8, 2873/5, 2874/8, 2875/9, 2876/8, 2878/9, 2880/11, 2882/7, 2884/12, 2886/7, 2887/7, 2889/9, 2894/6, 2895/7, 2897/4, 2899/5, 2900/3, 2905/12, 2906/7, 2910/11, 2912/8, 2915/5, 2918/9, 2922/7, 2932/12, 2945/9, 2949/10, 2950/11, 2951/9, 2953/4, 2954/9, 2956/7, 2957/9, 2958/6, 2959/6, 2960/6, 2961/8, 2973/6, 2987/9, 2989/11, 2990/11, 2991/8, 2994/8, 3004/10, 3005/7, 3017/7, 3026/10, 3029/A5, 3033/9, 3035/9, 3036/8, 3037/10, 3041/9, 3042/8, 3046/8, 3048/11, 3050/6, 3051/8, 3052/9, 3055/8, 3059/10, 3060/7, 3063/9, 3064/5, 3066/9, 3067/11, 3068/11, 3091/4, 3266/6, 3388/8, 3389/10, 3664/7, 3766/6, 3767/6, 3813/9, 4266/10
Pepys 2498: 1411.5/1, 1866.7/1, 2646.5/1, 2660.1/1, 2660.3/1, 2660.6/1, 3305.2/1, 3305.4/1, 3322.8/1, 3603.5/1
Pepys 2505: 2716/1a
Pepys 2553: 121.5/2, 199/3, 223/2, 232/3, 265/1, 276.5/1, 277/1, 293.5/2, 429/1, 442.5/1, 470.5/1, 515.5/1, 566/2, 649.8/2, 679.8/1, 704/7, 753.5/1, 758/1, 865.8/2, 886.5/2, 1148.5/1, 1264.5/2, 1330.5/2, 1356.5/2, 1370.5/1, 1470.8/1, 1503.5/1, 1527/2, 1587.3/2, 1599.5/2, 1640.5/2, 1820.5/1, 1820/3, 1855/1, 1934.5/2, 2018.5/2, 2032.5/2, 2072.8/1, 2143.5/1, 2161.5/1, 2226.5/1, 2247.5/1, 2289.8/1, 2349.3/2, 2349.5/2, 2349.8/1, 2354.3/1, 2457.5/2, 2465/2, 2551/1, 2587.5/1, 2619.8/2, 2621.5/2, 2623.3/2, 2632.5/1, 2697/1, 2818.8/2, 2820.5/1, 2821.3/2, 2821.5/2, 2831.2/2, 2834.5/1, 3077.5/2, 3116.5/2, 3117.3/1, 3117.5/2, 3117.7/2, 3117.8/2, 3118.6/1, 3118.8/2, 3190/3, 3243.3/1, 3248.5/1, 3256.6/2, 3306.8/2, 3496.3/2, 3556.5/2, 3598/2, 3634.3/2, 3634.6/2, 3646.3/2, 3660/2, 3694.6/2, 3768.3/2, 3768.6/2, 3776.5/1,

3845.5/1, 3860.8/1, 3870/2, 3908.5/1, 3942/1, 3954.5/1, 3960.5/2, 4005.5/2, 4095/3, 4110.8/2, 4116.5/2
Pepys 2833 (no number in *IMEV*): 727/C16a

Cambridge, Newnham College
4 (no number in *IMEV*): 620/1, 1459/B10, 3507/4

Cambridge, Pembroke College
32: 3272.5/1, 3273/12, 3900/1
82: 1267.5/1 **(MS 32 in *IMEV*), 1477.5/1 (MS 281 in *IMEV*)**
85 III: 417/1
120: 2233/13
243: 3185/2
248: 4220/2
258: 695/4, 738.5/1, 2162/1, 2320/A15, 3711.5/1, 3650/1
265: 3323/1
272: 3428/34
285: 1342/15, 1491/10, 2119/13, 2167/16, 4150/13
307: 2412/1, 2662/A10, 3809/1
folder of music fragments: 455.5/1
fragment of Piers Plowman (Kane A-text p.13): 1459/A11

Cambridge, Peterhouse
104: 706/2, 4165/1
134: 845/1
195: 3438.3/1
218: 3115.5/1
222: 4204/8*
255: 3175.5/1
257: 3918/1

Cambridge, Queens' College
12: 2229/16
13: 699/1, 1822/11, 4035/11

Cambridge, Sidney Sussex College
37: 529/3, 1050/2, 2556/2, 2812/3, 4243/2
39: 3514/1
55: 406/A5, 1342/17, 2119/15, 2167/18, 3685/4, 4150/14
63: 2662/B2, 3957/2
74: 3397/8
80: 1727/6
99: 106.5/1

Cambridge, St Catherine's College
7: 2662/A11

Cambridge, St John's College
15: 1943/1, 3965/1, 4088/3
28: 213/B2, 443/9, 791/11, 1546/9, 1801/2, 1859/11, 1911/10, 2707/1, 2717/1, 2724/1, 2755/9, 2960/7, 3384/6, 3452/5, 3559/1, 3706/1, 3973/4, 3997/2
29: 220/6, 3429/4
31: 4015/1
34: 1422.3/1, 2662/A12
37: 258/1, 906/5, 2004/1, 2620/1, 4184/5
62: 1977/2
71: 3102/2
80: 3428/35
111: 3211/2
112: 1857/1
127: 2320/B9, 3985/3
135: 518/1, 3265/1
137: 812/1, 3428/36
145: 1669/3
159: 142/B9, 191/5, 498/8, 594/6, 1003/10, 1127/6, 1141/7, 1150/7, 1204/7, 1223/7, 1321/5, 1822/7, 2001/A7, 2001/B8, 2002/7, 2058/6, 2077/6, 2114/7, 2283/5, 2298/8, 2329/9, 3081/8, 3133/6, 3254/7, 3273/7, 3275/7, 3282/9, 3287/7, 3339/7, 3350/6, 3408/7, 3463/6, 3802/7, 3863/10, 4151/8, 4156/4
176: 1342/16, 1491/11, 2119/14, 2167/17
179: 2320/B10
189: 239/8
191: 824/13, 3217/1, 3362/2
192: 3499/8
193: 966/1
195: 161/1, 3697/1
196: 1597/11
204: 399.5/1, 746.5/1, 1426.6/1, 1637.6/1, 2361.5/1, 2736.2/1, 2831.4/1, 3218.3/1, 4189.5/1
208: 2766/1
223: 2229/17
233: 1168/6*
234: 960.5/2
235: 285/1, 3327/7, 3657/1
237: 1538.5/1, 1664/1, 1708/2, 4264/2
256: 1030/2, 1101/3
259: 30/1, 352/2, 782/1, 972/1, 1484/1, 1492/1, 1744/1, 1900/1, 2098/3, 2339/2, 2735/1, 3098/1, 3214/1, 3312/1, 3329/1, 3594/1, 3654/1, 3931/1, 4078/1, 4241/1, 4256.3/1

Cambridge, Trinity College
43 (B.1.45): 445/2, 1917/1, 2285/2, 2286/1, 3998/1
61 (B.2.18): 220/7, 3958/1
108 (B.3.29): 1820/4
181 (B.15.39): 704/8, 1547.5/1, 4160/5
223 (B.10.12): 406/A6, 1732/1, 1780/1
257 (B.11.18): 588/1
263 (B.11.24): 824/14, 1823/2, 3805/1, 4060/1
305 (B.14.19): 248/2, 621.5/5, 879.5/5, 1727/7, 4110.5/5

(continued overleaf)

322 (B.14.38): 2017.5/15, 3397/3, 4056/14
323 (B.14.39): 98/1, 106/1, 109/1, 293/1, 426/1, 433/3, 522/1, 733.3/1, 747/1, 885/1, 912/1, 995/1, 1001.5/1, 1129/3, 1276.3/1, 1389.5/1, 1405/1, 1461/2, 1649/1, 1836/1, 1924/1, 1935/13, 1946/1, 1949/1, 2336/1, 2366/1, 2369/1, 2644/1, 2645/1, 2672/4, 2687/2, 2746/1, 2992/1, 2995/1, 3078/1, 3517/3, 3696/1, 3967/3, 4040.3/1, 4044/1, 4046/1, 4119/1, 4141/1, 4170/1, 4211/1
335 (B.14.52): 1272/3
353 (B.15.17): 611/1, 1459/B11
365 (B.15.30): 3122/3
366 (B.15.31): 237/1, 2364/3
367 (B.15.32): 1723/1
376 (B.15.40): 1286/5, 3687/6
432, wrong reference: 2742/5
536 (R.2.36): 1459/C17a
559 (R.2.59): 3502/3
581 (R.3.2): 2662/B3
582 (R.3.3): 4019/30
588 (R.3.8): 2153/3, 3976/3
593 (R.3.13): 245/17
594 (R.3.14): 964.5/1, 1459/A5
595 (R.3.15): 663/1, 3183/1, 3788/1, 3943/10, 4019/31, 4251/1
597 (R.3.17): 819.5/1, 2195/1, 4138/2
599 (R.3.19): 55/1, 71/4, 100/A6, 190.5/1, 267/1, 437/1, 590/2, 671/2, 928.5/1, 935/5, 1086/3, 1168/7*, 1172.5/1, 1238/1, 1300/1, 1528/1, 1562/1, 1592/1, 1838/1, 1944/2, 2128/1, 2148/1, 2254/1, 2311/1, 2384.8/1, 2464/4, 2478.5/1, 2510/1, 2524/1, 2541/1, 2588.5/1, 2624/4, 2625/6, 2661/1, 2756/5, 2767/1, 2784/5, 3197/1, 3258/1, 3412/12, 3493/1, 3761/1, 3807/1, 3983/1, 4005/1, 4178/2, 4205/1, 4230/3, 4231/1
600 (R.3.20): 92/2, 120/2, 131/2, 154/1, 355/3, 439/3, 458/1, 464/1, 500/1, 614/1, 653/3, 666/7, 674/4, 809/9, 869/1, 870/1, 913/5, 970/2, 1168/8*, 1419/1, 1498/1, 1872/1, 1905/3, 1928/1, 1955.5/2, 2210/1, 2211/2, 2212/1, 2213/1, 2541/2, 2572/1, 2592/2, 2688/1, 3065/3, 3190/4, 3301/1, 3327/C, 3348/3, 3521/2, 3523/1, 3542/7, 3604/1, 3606/1, 3611/2, 3655/2, 3661/7, 3670/C, 3718/1, 4245/4, 4260/2
601 (R.3.21): 168/1, 178/2, 357/1, 401/5, 447/3, 464/2, 533/1, 561/3, 704/9, 723/1, 875/2, 899/1, 1019/2, 1037/1, 1045/1, 1056/1, 1152/1, 1236/1, 1294/5, 1439/1, 1720/2, 1854/4, 1865/4, 1874/1, 2081/3, 2156/2, 2218/2, 2323/2, 2345/2, 2392/1, 2413/3, 2493/1, 2556/3, 2570/1, 2574/13, 2579/1, 2591/4, 2592/3, 2711/1, 2714/5, 2791/8, 3129/1, 3443/3, 3543/1, 3632/18, 3651/1, 3673/2, 3798/4, 4122/2, 4243/3, 4246/6, 4249/3
602 (R.3.22): 2229/18, 2574/14, 2742/6
603 (R.3.23): 245/18
605 (R.3.25): 56/6, 57/6, 58/6, 59/6, 74/1, 82/9, 184/8, 201/8, 213/B3, 443/10, 586/1, 721/9, 791/12, 907/6, 1546/10, 1801/3, 1809/9, 1859/12, 1911/11, 2127/7, 2304/9, 2707/2, 2717/2, 2755/10, 2837/2, 2839/11, 2841/2, 2842/9, 2843/10, 2844/11, 2848/8, 2850/11, 2854/13, 2856/9, 2858/9, 2860/10, 2862/4, 2866/12, 2867/3, 2868/10, 2870/5, 2872/9, 2873/6, 2874/9, 2875/10, 2876/9, 2878/10, 2880/12, 2882/8, 2883/4, 2884/13, 2886/8, 2887/8, 2889/10, 2894/7, 2895/8, 2897/5, 2899/6, 2900/4, 2905/13, 2906/8, 2910/12, 2912/9, 2915/6, 2918/10, 2922/8, 2932/13, 2945/10, 2949/11, 2950/12, 2951/10, 2954/10, 2956/8, 2957/10, 2959/7, 2960/8, 2961/9, 2973/7, 2987/10, 2989/12, 2990/12, 2991/9, 3004/11, 3005/8, 3017/8, 3026/11, 3029/A6, 3033/10, 3035/10, 3037/11, 3041/10, 3042/9, 3046/9, 3048/12, 3050/7, 3051/9, 3052/10, 3053/2, 3055/9, 3059/11, 3060/8, 3063/10, 3064/6, 3066/10, 3067/12, 3068/12, 3091/5, 3159/2, 3266/7, 3349/1, 3384/7, 3388/9, 3389/11, 3452/6, 3559/2, 3813/10, 3973/5, 4266/11, 4267/3
652 (R.4.20): 1032/2, 1310/1, 2440/1, 3196/2, 3297/1, 3308/1, 3928/9
655 (R.4.26): 727/B10
759 (R.7.23): 3754/4
899 (R.14.26): 1263/1
905 (R.14.32): 417.8/1
910 (R.14.38): 3772/9
911 (R.14.39): 1408/1
913 (R.14.41): 2766.2/1
915 (R.14.44): 2614/1
916 (R.14.45): 1214/1, 2656/18
921 (R.14.51): 1496.3/1, 2627/5, 3158/1, 3190/5, 3348/4, 3848/8
1037 (O.1.13): 3422/4, 3578/2, 3848/9, 3919.5/1
1041 (O.1.17): 2320/A8
1053 (O.1.29): 826/1, 2017.5/16, 4056/15
1081 (O.1.57): 1502/5
1105 (O.2.1): 2164/1

1109 (O.2.5): 3104.5/1
1117 (O.2.13): 824/47, 2627/6, 2726/1, 3405.3/1
1119 (O.2.15): 1276/8, 3249/13, 3257/4, 3772/10
1120 (O.2.16): 595/13, 2656/19, 3721/7
1137 (O.2.33): 659/1, 1203/1, 1214/2, 2826/3
1144 (O.2.40): 733.8/1, 806/1, 871/1, 1442.5/1, 2753/1, 3866/1
1149 (O.2.45): 3318.8/2, 3502.5/1, 3792.5/3, 3894.6/2, 3927.6/1, 4079.8/1
1157 (O.2.53): 726/1, 734.8/2, 769/2, 906/19, 960.3/1, 1176.5/1, 1255/1, 1585.8/1, 1730/1, 2261.2/1, 2507/2, 3308.5/1, 3318.4/3, 3538/2, 3672/1, 3793/2, 3905/1, 4035/12, 4129/4, 4148/6, 4212/1, 4254.5/2, 4255/3, 4285/1
1174 (O.3.2): 4183/2
1184 (O.3.12): 1842.5/1
1209 (O.3.37): 4214.5/1
1212 (O.3.40): 935/6
1230 (O.3.58): 21/3, 88/2, 111/2, 354/3, 1471/4, 1473/2, 2315/1, 2665/1, 2716/2, 3385/2, 3536/1, 3574/2, 3776/3
1269 (O.4.39): 3772/11
1283 (O.5.2): 1515/1, 2516/10, 3928/10
1287 (O.5.6): 2147/2
1312 (O.5.31): 595/14
1359 (O.7.31): 3515/1
1413 (O.9.1): 979/4
1434 (O.9.22): 945.5/1
1438 (O.9.26): 2698/7, 4113/10
1440 (O.9.28): 3848/10
1450 (O.9.38): 199/4, 240/1, 561/4, 562/3, 1454/2, 1502/10, 1703/14, 1944/3, 2519/1, 3068.5/1, 3170/1, 3416.5/1, 3420/2, 3424/2, 3715/1, 4014.5/1, 4083/2, 4090/2, 4102/1, 4106/1, 4146/1, 4189/1, 4202/2
1652: 3327/G
unidentified: 3118.4/1

Cambridge, Trinity Hall
16: 3648/1

Cambridge, Univ. Lib.
Add.2585: 264/2, 550.5/1, 816/2, 995.2/1, 1393.5/1, 2449/2, 2723.5/1, 2883/6, 3036/12, 3142/2
Add.2604: 3545/1
Add.2750: 3461.5/1
Add.2764: 2636.5/1
Add.2793: 100/A4a
Add.2794: 3412/9a
Add.2823: 245/15
Add.3039: 50/3, 56/3, 57/3, 58/3, 59/3, 184/6, 721/6, 728/3, 1788/3, 2304/6, 2839/8, 2848/6, 2850/8, 2866/9, 2870/3, 2873/4, 2875/8, 2876/6, 2878/7, 2882/5, 2886/6, 2887/6, 2894/5, 2896/3, 2897/3, 2899/4, 2912/6, 2918/7, 2922/5, 2932/10 **(Add.3029 in *IMEV*)**, 2945/7, 2950/9, 2951/7, 2954/8, 2957/7, 2958/5, 2961/7, 2974/1, 2987/7, 2991/6, 2994/6, 3005/6, 3029/B4, 3033/8, 3037/8, 3041/7, 3046/6, 3048/9, 3050/5, 3052/7, 3055/6, 3059/8, 3063/7, 3064/13, 3066/7, 3067/9, 3068/9, 3204/1, 3266/4, 3389/8, 3813/7, 4266/8
Add.3042: 1273.5/1 **(Add.3402 in *IMEV*)**, 3760.5/2
Add.3137: 3928/7
Add.3573: 1597/10
Add.4026: 2698/11a, 4113/16a
Add.4120: 1155/1
Add.4122: 1835/1, 2447/1, 2672/3
Add.4325: 1459/C8
Add.4407 (19)a–c: 205/1
Add.4407 (19)d–f: 1114/2
Add.4407 (19)g: 2685.5/1
Add.4407 (19)h: 2078/2
Add.4407 (27): 3339.8/1
Add.4544: 306.3/1
Add.5943: 352/1, 438/1, 453/1, 662/1, 670/1, 707/1, 939/1, 1293.5/2, 1347/2, 1415/1, 2135/1, 2138/1, 2738/1, 3280/2, 3418/1, 3596/2, 3662/1, 3806/1, 3892/1, 4218/1
Add.6150: 1342/37, 1491/25, 2119/51, 2167/44, 4150/32
Add.6686: 1740/1, 3632/15, 3745/1, 4184/16
Add.6693: 1781/17, 3428/92
Add.6860: 1474/2, 1820/10
Add.6864: 3928/22
Add.6865 (olim Gurney): 2167/38
Add.7350 (1): 1344.5/1, 2635.5/1, 3328.5/1, 3443.5/1
Add.8335 (olim Bute): 25/12, 26/13, 32/10, 40/7, 42/3, 43/6, 45/10, 46/9, 47/10, 79/8, 89/8, 97/10, 132/7, 284/10, 286/10, 288/8, 289/12, 290/6, 291/9, 306/10, 314/11, 385/4, 416/6, 485/9, 749/3, 1117/7, 1118/8, 1136/8, 1464/10, 1482/12, 1494/9, 1518/5, 1519/9, 1521/8, 1641/8, 1642/10, 1643/11, 1645/8, 1646/9, 1647/9, 1648/8, 1657/8, 1862/7, 1912/7, 2084/7, 2094/8, 2301/8, 2859/6, 2908/3, 2926/6, 2927/6, 2930/8, 2933/2, 2935/6, 2936/8, 2937/9, 2938/7, 2939/8, 2941/5, 2942/2, 2965/4, 2967/6, 2968/6, 2970/8, 2971/9, 2976/8, 2978/7, 2996/10, 2999/6, 3002/8, 3003/9, 3009/8, 3012/8, 3013/7, 3018/11, 3019/2, 3020/7, 3021/8, 3288/8, 3290/9,

(continued overleaf)

(continued overleaf)

Cambridge, Univ. Lib.

197.5/1, 445/1, 457/1, 514/1, 607.8/1, 633/1, 825.5/1, 835/1 **(Gg.3.8 in *IMEV*),** 873.5/1, 1009/1, 1134/1, 1265.5/1, 1301/1, 1406/1, 1428/1 **(Gg.3.8 in *IMEV*),** 1478/1, 1493.5/1, 1611/1, 1625/1, 1803/1, 2046/1 **(Gg.3.8 in *IMEV*),** 2077.5/1, 2085/1, 2502/1, 2602.6/1, 2811.8/1, 3292/1, 3293/1, 3302/1, 3355/2, 3397/1, 3563/1 **(Gg.3.8 in *IMEV*),** 3699/1, 4040.6/1, 4056.3/1, 4091.6/1, 4094.8/1, 4240/1, 4193/1 **(Gg.3.8 in *IMEV*),** 4263/1

Ii.3.21: 28/2, 3661/5
Ii.3.26: 1913/10, 3943/7, 4019/28, 4117/2, 4154/3
Ii.4.9: 215/1, 705/1, 778/2, 976/1, 1188/3, 1323/1, 1901/1, 1907/8, 2017.5/12, 2045/1, 2059/1, 2062/1, 2314/1, 2780/4, 4056/11, 4068/1, 4154/4
Ii.4.11: 24/1, 463/1
Ii.5.41: 33/2
Ii.6.2: 1729/1, 3427/1
Ii.6.4: 4058.8/1, 4126/1
Ii.6.11: 3943/8, 4018/1
Ii.6.36: 430.5/1
Ii.6.39: 2040/1, 2492/1
Ii.6.40: 2320/C5
Ii.6.43: 241/3, 1027/1, 1341/1, 1370/2, 1687/1, 1727/5, 1971/1, 2119/37, 2577/5, 3233/2, 3241/3
Ii.6.44: 4184/3
Ii.6.55: 2017.5/13, 4056/12
Kk.1.3: 2229/13, 2553/II.1, 2574/10, 4019/69
Kk.1.5: 120.7/1, 450/1, 687/1, 809/7, 2235/1, 3130/1, 3151/1, 3154/1, 3362/1, 3466/1, 3665/2, 4008/A2, 4029/2, 4100/1
Kk.1.6: 186/2, 253/1, 401/3, 915/2, 1025/1, 1683.3/1, 1719/7, 2081/2, 2428/8, 2784/4, 2791/6, 2802/1, 2833/1, 3184/1, 3845/7
Kk.1.7: 233/8, 263/8, 540/6, 1242/8, 1243/7, 1244/8, 1245/7, 1246/8, 1247/8, 1249/8, 1296/7
Kk.5.30: 298.5/A1, 298.5/B2, 1367.1/1, 2516/9
Kk.6.16: 757/1, 2515/1
Kk.6.18: 1007/1
Kk.6.30: 595/11, 865.5/1, 1356/1
Ll.1.8: 11.5/1, 245/14, 918.5/1
Ll.1.11: 2733/2
Ll.1.18: 308.5/1
Ll.2.17: 3428/31
Ll.4.14: 71/3, 296.3/1, 1459/B8, 1686/1, 4128/1
Ll.5.10: 121.5/1, 293.5/1, 541.5/1, 566/1, 649.8/1, 704/6, 861.5/1, 865.8/1, 886.5/1, 1264.5/1, 1330.5/1, 1356.5/1, 1373.5/1, 1444.5/1, 1527/1, 1587.3/1, 1599.5/1, 1640.5/1, 1820/13, 1934.5/1, 2018.5/1, 2032.5/1, 2244.3/1, 2258.5/1, 2267/1, 2349.3/1, 2349.5/1, 2457.5/1, 2465/1, 2619.8/1, 2621.5/1, 2623.3/1, 2821.3/1, 2821.5/1, 2831.2/1, 3077.5/1, 3116.5/1, 3117.5/1, 3117.7/1, 3117.8/1, 3118.8/1, 3140.5/1, 3256.6/1, 3306.8/1, 3496.3/1, 3556.5/1, 3595.3/1, 3598/1, 3634.3/1, 3634.6/1, 3646.3/1, 3660/4, 3694.6/1, 3768.3/1, 3768.6/1, 3870/1, 3960.5/1, 4005.5/1, 4095/2, 4110.8/1, 4116.5/1, 4165.5/1
Ll.5.18: 439/2
Mm.1.15: 4204/6*
Mm.1.18: 2360/1
Mm.1.35: 582/1
Mm.2.5: 1913/11, 4019/29
Mm.2.21: 2662/A9
Mm.3.21: 4204/7*
Mm.4.28: 2988/4
Mm.4.41: 1565/1, 3475/1, 4264.5/1
Mm.4.42: 738/1, 2130/1
Mm.5.14: 1583/2
Mm.6.5: 2574/11
Mm.6.17: 2320/B16
Nn.4.12: 130.5/1
Oo.7.32: 3408/12

Cambridge, Mass., Harvard Univ., Houghton Lib.

***27282.67.10**: 2590/7
Eng.515: 3428/82
Eng.530: 875/6, 2714/12, 4186.5/2
Eng.532F: 2229/26a
Eng.590 (530 in *IMEV*): 2615/3
Eng.752: 2516/21
Eng.1031: 1907/12
Eng.1032: 1645/11
Eng.1054: 710/14
Richardson 22: 454.5/1, 1732.5/1, 4154/8, 4184/17
Transcript by Sir F. Madden: 1853/1a

Cambridge, Mass., Harvard Univ., Widener Lib.

1 (olim Brough Hall): 4204/11*

Campbell, Robinson Cat.74 1944, no. 268, now Boston Public Lib. f.med.94

Canterbury, Cathedral Lib.

Add.68: 1807/1, 1808/1, 3448.8/1, 3675/1, 3810.3/1
Charta Antiqua M 251: 3300/6
Christchurch letters, vol.2, 173: 150/1

Christchurch letters, vol.2, **174**:
3271/1
Fragment (not located): 1120/2
**Inscription in inventory (not
located)**: 938/1, 942/1
Lit.D.13: 3428/54
Lit.D.14: 1204/14, 1935/15
Memorandum (not located): 2538/2
Register J: 2698/9, 4113/13
Register P: 2698/10, 4113/14

Cardiff, Public Lib.
3.174: 400/8, 621/8, 1490/8,
2340/8, 3496/7, 3518/8

Charlottesville, Univ. of Virginia
Hench 10 (no number in *IMEV*):
3428/87

Chatsworth, Duke of Devonshire
**Canterbury Tales, now privately
owned**: 4019/12
**Lydgate, Life of Margaret, now Tokyo,
Takamiya 24**
fragment of Canterbury Tales:
4019/61

Chester, Company of Coopers
Enrolment Book: 716/9

Chicago, Newberry Lib.
32.9 (olim Helmingham Hall LJ II.1):
3428/76
33.3 (olim Rosenbach 475): 1168/21
= also 1168/29
C 19169: 3428/85
D 26986 (=Ricci Ry8): 8/1, 1747/3
Gen. Lib. Add.8: 1596.8/1, 1597/22
Gen. Lib. Add.12: 1172/5
**Louis H. Silver 1 (2 in *IMEV*, Ricci
Sup. p.176)**: 4019/64
Louis H. Silver 3: 2662/A24
Louis H. Silver 4: 1168/35
**f.33.7 (olim Merton 28, Breslauer
Cat.90 item 24)**: 2229/39

Chicago, Univ. Lib.
564: 4019/52
565: 1168/24
566: 2574/39, 2742/13

Chichester, W. Sussex Record Office
Cowfold Churchwarden's Accounts:
560/4

Cleveland, Ohio, Public Lib.
**W.90.91.92.C.468 (olim Aldenham,
Goldschmidt Cat.55 item 59)**:
1881/10

Cook-Davis (=Davies-Cooke)
**Sotheby 15 June 1959, lot 205, now
San Marino, Huntington HM 19916**

Copenhagen, Royal Lib.
Gl. kgl. S. 248 2°: 1241.5/1
Gl. kgl. S. 3500 8°: 2403.3/1,
3249/31
Thott 110 4°: 1359/1 (**Thott 29264**
in *IMEV*), 1640/3 (**29264** in *IMEV*),
4181/11, 4230/8 (**29264** in *IMEV*)
Thott 304 2° (no number in *IMEV*):
1597/20
Thott 306 2°: 3957/3

Coughton Court
**Sarum Manual from Buckland House,
Christie 20 Dec 1972 (not sold)**:
4204/12*

Coventry, City Record Office
11/2 (Robert Croo MS): 4248/1
Acc.325/1: 124/6, 239/14,
248.5/1, 299/5, 502.5/1, 809/22,
1561/8, 1881/11, 2229/45, 2262/2,
2591/7, 3121/8, 3190/15, 3348/10,
3582/6, 3787/12, 3928/29
Leet Book, BA/E/F/37/1: 466/1,
1075/1, 1665/1, 2781/1, 2834/1,
3322/1, 3881/1

Cox
privately owned: 906/21, 2039.3/3,
3306/3

**Deritend House, now Stafford, Staffs
Record Office, Bagot D1721/3/186**:
3529/1

**Douai Abbey, Woolhampton, Berks
7 (no number in *IMEV*)**: 3428/94

**Dublin, Christ Church Cathedral
Vellum Account Roll 1337–1346,
burned in 1922**: 2741/1

**Dublin, National Lib. of Ireland
D 1435 (olim Kilkenny Castle)**:
1010/1, 2774/1

Dublin, Trinity College
67: 1197.3/1
69: 2631.5/1, 3429/15
70: 255/2, 620/4, 1758/2, 1983/2
76: 245/33
83: 4154.5/1
97: 734.5/3
155: 197.8/6, 484/2, 1367.5/7,
1700/1, 1717/1, 1743/1, 2017.5/23,
3238/6, 4056/2
156: 1961/9, 3428/65
157: 3428/66, 3707.8/1
158: 1139/5, 2245/1, 3428/67
159: 1342/31, 1491/19, 1998/2,
2119/27, 2167/36, 4150/27
160: 1270.2/3, 1333/3, 1540/7,
2347/4, 3226/4

(continued overleaf)

Dublin, Trinity College

211: 1326.5/1, 2708.5/1, 3305.6/1
212: 1459/C15
213: 1458/3, 3947.3/2
214: 1201/1, 1498.5/1
277: 265.5/1, 541.8/3, 830/3, 834/3, 847/3, 1140/3, 1271/3, 1332/3, 1551/3, 1975/3, 2256/3
301: 3211/6
312: 3200.5/1, 4036.5/1
319: 3569/1
340: 430.5/6
351: 1286/8, 1342/32, 1491/20, 2119/28, 2167/37
389: 3249/28
423: 245/34, 553.5/1, 1197.4/1, 3926.5/1
432: 158.4/1, 455/1, 508/1, 700/2, 1380/1, 1585.5/1, 1924.5/1, 1931.8/1, 2446.5/1, 2609/1, 2617/1, 2742/11, 3190/12, 3636/1, 3638.3/1, 3784.6/1, 3856.5/1, 3966/1, 4120.6/1
490: 1934/6
500: 763/1
509: 3793/7
516: 324/9, 734.8/8, 824/39, 1032/5, 1409.8/1, 1555/3, 1934/7, 2262.3/1, 2727/1, 3113/4, 3143.5/1, 3451/1 **(no number in *IMEV*)**, 3618.5/1, 3632/37, 3943/16, 3987/1, 4018/5, 4029/15, 4030.5/1, 4150.6/1, 4181/16
517: 906/13
519: 854/27
537: 824/40, 4112/6
641: 871.5/1
652: 2363/1
661: 1817.5/1, 2451.5/3, 3567.3/1
662: 2284.3/1
684: 3772/22

Dunrobin Castle, Duke of Sutherland
Fearn Calendar, deposited at National Lib. of Scotland: 1423/1, 4115/1

Durham, Cathedral Lib.
A.III.12: 4088/5
A.IV.25: 2174/1
B.III.34: 4053/2
B.IV.19: 1218.5/1
Prior's Kitchen, Archid. Dunelm. 60: 2741.5/1
Prior's Kitchen, Bp Hatfield's Survey: 2820.3/1
Prior's Kitchen, Registrum parvum II: 2578.5/1

Durham, Univ. Lib.
Cosin V.i.9: 239/15
Cosin V.i.12: 1640/2
Cosin V.ii.13: 666/9, 2297/1, 3306.3/1, 3327/14, 3941.5/1
Cosin V.ii.14: 439/7, 854/25, 3156/3, 3928/18, 3955/15
Cosin V.ii.15: 1597/17
Cosin V.ii.16: 2574/32
Cosin V.iii.9: 95.8/1, 124/4, 299/4, 430.5/4, 484.5/1, 512.5/4, 513/5, 859.5/1, 1151/11, 1173/5, 1218.8/1, 1294.3/1, 1436.2/1, 1561/7, 1717.3/1, 1829/2, 1923.5/1, 2291.5/1, 2607.5/1, 2617.5/1, 3121/6, 3135.5/1, 3171.5/1, 3318.3/1, 3361.6/1, 3582/5, 3612.5/1, 3639.5/1, 3917.5/1, 4072/7, 4073.3/1, 4096.5/1, 4098.1/1
Cosin V.iii.10: 378.5/1, 3848/23
Cosin V.iii.11: 3327/H
Cosin V.iii.24: 2469.5/1
Cosin V.iv.2: 142/B10, 400/9, 498/9, 565/7, 1204/8, 2329/10, 2775/8, 3287/8, 3408/8
Cosin V.iv.4: 2300.8/1
Cosin V.v.12: 3452.3/1
Cosin V.v.15: 2320/A12
Cosin V.v.19: 1561.5/1, 1640/4, 3318.2/1

Dyson Perrins 33, Sotheby 29 Nov 1960, lot 109, now San Marino, Huntington HM 19999

Dyson Perrins, Sotheby Dec 1958, lot 42, now San Marino, Huntington HM 30313

Earl Fitzwilliam, now Oxford, Bodleian, Duke Humfrey 2

Edinburgh, College of Physicians
Cursor mundi, Northern Homily Cycle: 26/11, 45/8, 97/8, 104/3, 284/8, 306/8, 323/7, 777/5, 1494/7, 1642/8, 1885/3, 2153/8, 2920.5/1, 2920/3, 2930/6, 2996/8, 3012/6, 3018/9, 3021/6, 3208/3, 3290/7, 3317/8, 3395/6, 3399/3, 3492/6, 3740/6, 3789/4, 3790/6, 3857/5, 3954/8, 3976/7, 4226/7

Edinburgh, National Lib. of Scotland
651: 399/6, 1377/6
6128: 1295.8/1 (should be 2755.5)
Advocates 1.1.6: 121.5/3, 158.7/1, 199/10, 223/3, 228/1, 265/2, 277/2, 293.5/3, 417.5/1, 429/2, 442.5/2, 470.5/3, 479.5/1, 512.8/1, 515.5/2, 612/1, 648/2, 666/8, 674/7, 679.8/2, 679/2, 688.3/1, 688.5/1, 753.3/1, 758/2, 765.3/1,

767/2, 824/34, 861.5/2, 865.8/3, 886.5/3, 952/2, 1021/1, 1048.5/1, 1119.3/1, 1148.5/2, 1264.5/3, 1270.2/2, 1330.5/3, 1355/2, 1370.5/2, 1409.3/2, 1422.1/1, 1440.5/1, 1503.5/2, 1527/3, 1554/1, 1587.3/3, 1598.3/1, 1598/1, 1640.5/3, 1657.5/1, 1820/7, 1855/2, 2013/2, 2018.5/3, 2072.8/2, 2139/1, 2143.5/2, 2226.5/2, 2244/1, 2277.3/1, 2289.8/2, 2306.5/1, 2312.5/1, 2354.3/2, 2420/1, 2451.5/2, 2497.5/1, 2517/1, 2520/1, 2523.5/1, 2551/2, 2574/29, 2579.5/1, 2580/1, 2621.5/3, 2623.3/3, 2632.5/2, 2634/1, 2820.5/2, 2820/5, 2821.3/4, 2821.5/3, 2831.2/3, 2831.6/1, 2831/1, 3051.5/1, 3079.7/1, 3087/8, 3117.8/3, 3118.8/3, 3140.5/2, 3151/2, 3183/2, 3190/10, 3225.5/1, 3226/1, 3256.6/3, 3306.8/3, 3327/D, 3442/1, 3477.3/1, 3498/1, 3556.5/3, 3598/3, 3599/1, 3634.3/3, 3634.6/3, 3648.8/1, 3660/3, 3695/2, 3701.5/1, 3703/2, 3727/2, 3751.5/1, 3768.3/3, 3776.5/3, 3860.8/2, 3866.5/1, 3870/3, 3908.5/2, 3911.5/1, 3942/2, 3946.5/1, 3960.5/3, 3990.5/1, 4005.3/1, 4083/3, 4095/4, 4112.5/1, 4116.5/3, 4116/1, 4237/1

Advocates 18.1.7 (no number in *IMEV*): 1965.5/1

Advocates 18.2.8: 2221/2

Advocates 18.4.4: 442/1, 591/1, 3600/1

Advocates 18.7.21: 7/1, 23/1, 33.6/1, 91/3, 94/1, 156/1, 162/1, 193.8/1, 197/1, 221/2, 222.5/1, 230.5/1, 327/1, 352/4, 353/2, 424/1, 441/1, 461/1, 468/1, 480/1, 494/1, 499/1, 501/1, 504/1, 517.5/1, 526/1, 554/1, 593/1, 602/1, 607.5/1, 609/1, 628/1, 629/1, 634/1, 703/1, 825.8/1, 829/1, 873/1, 955/1, 1002/1, 1061/1, 1089/1, 1129/7, 1139/3, 1167/1 **(18.7.12 in *IMEV*)**, 1210.5/1, 1220/1, 1262/1, 1274/1, 1336/1, 1337/1, 1431/1, 1432/1, 1436/1, 1472/1, 1523/2, 1606/1, 1610/1, 1636/1, 1714/1, 1737/1, 1847/2, 1864/1, 1942/1, 1965/1, 2001/B11, 2006/1, 2011/1, 2012/1, 2023/1, 2024/2, 2036/1, 2066.8/1, 2074/3, 2083/1, 2095/1, 2155/2, 2234/1, 2240/2, 2258/1, 2260/1, 2289.5/1, 2298/12, 2341/1, 2708/1, 2743.5/1, 2762/1, 2817/2, 3078.5/1, 3079.3/1, 3100.5/1, 3109/1, 3111/1, 3245/1, 3264/1, 3277/1, 3356/1, 3452.8/1, 3464/1, 3485/1, 3500/1, 3505/1, 3510.5/1, 3516.5/1, 3520/1, 3562/1, 3567.6/1, 3678/1, 3690/1, 3691/1, 3764/1, 3783/1, 3825/1, 3846/1, 3862/1, 3903/1, 3908/1, 3969/5, 4084/1, 4088/6, 4110.3/1, 4159/1, 4221/2, 4222/1, 4225/1, 4256.5/1, 4263/2, 4286/1

Advocates 18.8.1: 1179/1

Advocates 18.8.5: 929/1

Advocates 19.1.2: 1040/1a

Advocates 19.1.11: 1308/1, 1890/2, 2229/36, 3985/8

Advocates 19.2.1 (Auchinleck): 185/2, 203/1, 206/1, 209/3, 213/B5, 282.5/1, 303.6/1, 304.5/1, 351/7, 552.8/1, 683/2, 821/4, 823.3/1, 946/1, 1101/9, 1103/1, 1105/C5, 1108/3, 1140.5/1, 1159/1, 1382/1, 1614/1, 1675/1, 1754/1, 1760/1, 1840/3, 1857/2, 1873.5/1A, 1895/6, 1956/1, 1979/7A, 1993/A4, 2253/1, 2288.8/4, 2602.3/1, 3145/3, 3187/A5, 3222/2, 3310/5, 3452/10, 3462/1, 3868/3, 3869/1, 3997/6, 4119.5/1, 4150.3/1, 4165/2

Advocates 19.2.2: 2701/1, 3217/2

Advocates 19.2.3: 399/4, 1377/4

Advocates 19.2.4: 399/5, 1377/5

Advocates 19.2.5: 548.5/1

Advocates 19.3.1: 64/1, 172/4, 340/2, 358/1, 374/4 **(19.31.1 in *IMEV*)**, 378/2, 467.5/1, 674/8, 707/2, 973/2, 1032/4, 1116/1, 1184/7, 1446/2, 1448/3, 1724/4, 1772/1, 1781/11, 1920/6, 2157/5, 2574/30, 2714/9, 3083/4, 3087/9, 3088/5, 3184/3, 3435/1, 3507/7, 3518.5/1, 3627/4, 4153/2, 4230/7

Advocates 23.7 11: 3453/9

Advocates 34.7.3: 856/1, 1429/1, 1509/1, 2055/1, 3612/5, 3774/1

Advocates b.44.2, not identified: 2085/2

Edinburgh, Scottish Record Office GD5/26/48, Fordun's Chronicle, on deposit from Brechin Castle, Earl of Dalhousie: 1181/2

Edinburgh, Univ. Lib.

27: 839/1

42: 4124/1

82: 142/A7, 191/6, 400/10, 495/5, 498/10, 565/8, 594/7, 621/9, 1127/7, 1141/8, 1150/8, 1204/9, 1223/8, 1490/9, 1822/8, 1935/8,

(continued overleaf)

Edinburgh, Univ. Lib.
2001/A8, 2002/8, 2058/7, 2114/8, 2283/6, 2298/9, 2329/11, 2340/9, 2596/6, 2729/6, 2775/9, 2832/6, 3081/9, 3133/7, 3147/6, 3254/8, 3273/8, 3275/8, 3287/9, 3339/8, 3350/7, 3408/9, 3463/7, 3496/8, 3518/9, 3649/5, 3716/6, 3802/8, 3863/11, 4143/8, 4156/5, 4239/6
114: 1759/2, 2118/2, 3027/5, 3231/6, 3241/6
186: 1181/1, 1824.4/2, 2685.8/2, 3168.6/1, 4247/3
202: 2229/37
205: 254/1, 612/2, 648/3, 824/35, 1065/1, 1119/3, 1376/1, 1598/2, 2057/1, 2557/1, 2831.8/2, 3703/3, 3942/3
218: 1873.5/2, 1979/7B
521: 417.5/2a, 1119.3/2a, 2461/2a
Dc.1.43 (Ruthven MS): 285/2, 1842.5/3
Dk.7.49 (Elphinston MS): 1842.5/2
La.III.164 (Laing 164 in *IMEV*): 595/18
La.III.431 (listed as olim Laing): 399/5B
La.III.450/1: 276.5/3a, 636/1a **(Laing 450* in *IMEV*)**, 1082.5/1a, 1507/8a **(Laing 450* in *IMEV*)**, 1554/2a **(Laing 450* in *IMEV*)**, 2289.8/3a, 3703/4a
La.III.481: 3187/D1A
La.IV.27: 54/1a, 276.5/3b, 303.3/1a
La.IV.28: 3187/D1b

Erfurt, Stadtbibl.
Amplon Oct. 58: 1422/2, 4129/7

Esopus, New York, Mount St Alphonsus Seminary
1: 2577/15

Eton College
34: 142/B11, 1003/11, 1204/10, 1935/9
36: 196/1
98: 3551/1

Geneva, Bibl. Bodmer
48: 4019/54
110 (olim Harmsworth, Sotheby Oct 1945, lot 1963): 2516/20
178 (olim Gurney 121): 2662/C9
Romances, now Princeton, Taylor Medieval 9

Ghent, Univ. Lib.
317: 2788/1, 3351/1, 3408/14, 4053.5/1

Glasgow, Univ. Lib.
Hunterian 5: 1168/17
Hunterian 7: 2662/A21
Hunterian 83: 182/1, 399.5/8, 746.5/7, 889/3, 1426.6/7, 1637.6/8, 2361.5/8, 2376/1, 2736.2/8, 2831.4/8, 3218.3/8, 4189.5/7
Hunterian 89: 245/30
Hunterian 104: 654/4
Hunterian 197: 1913/22, 4019/41
Hunterian 230: 77/5, 106.5/3, 1162.9/1, 1628.8/1, 2056/3, 2318/1
Hunterian 232: 2574/33, 2742/8
Hunterian 239: 239/12, 1151.5/1
Hunterian 258: 3848/24
Hunterian 259: 824/36, 854/26, 3955/16
Hunterian 388: 2129/1
Hunterian 400: 710/9, 1151/12
Hunterian 409: 1297/7, 2092/1
Hunterian 415: 727/A6
Hunterian 472: 3499/10
Hunterian 512: 611/2, 1747/2, 3499/11
Hunterian 520: 1781/12

Gloucester, Cathedral Lib.
5: 2516/16

Goldschmidt Cat.71 1943, no.1, now Tokyo, Takamiya 65

Gorhambury
Orosius manuscript (*IMEV* says location unknown): 2403.5/1, 2548.5/1

Göttingen, Univ. Lib.
Histor.740: 1559/1
Philol.163 n: 854/32, 3955/19
Theol.107: 694/5, 780/3, 788/4, 959/3, 1029/1, 1775/3, 1786/4, 1885/4, 2153/9, 3208/4, 3976/8

Greg, Goldschmidt Cat.71, 1943, item 1, now Tokyo, Takamiya 65

Grenoble, Bibl. municipale
873 (no number in *IMEV*, 4014/1 numbered in *SUP*): 134/1, 158/1, 844/1, 922/2, 2176/1, 2567/3, 3162/1, 4014/1, 4256/1

Gribbel, John, Philadelphia (Ricci p.2112) now Berkeley 75

Gurney 121, now Geneva, Bodmer 178

Gurney, now British Lib. Egerton 3245

Gurney, now Cambridge Univ.Lib. Add.6865

Halliwell, Sotheby 1920, lot 515, now Cambridge, Mass., Harvard, Houghton Lib. Eng.515

Harmsworth, Rolle, now Beeleigh Abbey

Harmsworth, Sotheby Oct 1945, lot 1963, now Geneva, Bodmer 110

Hastings Ashby-de-la-Zouche, Quaritch Cat, now New York, Pierpont Morgan M125

Hatfield House, Marquess of Salisbury
C.F. & E.P. Box S/1 (no number in *IMEV*): 3327/I
C.P.270 (no number in *IMEV*): 233/10, 263/10, 540/8, 1242/10, 1243/9, 1244/10, 1245/9, 1246/10, 1247/10, 1248/9, 1249/10, 1296/9, 1719/9, 2428/10

Helmingham Hall
LJ I.7, now London Univ. Lib. 657
LJ I.10, now Tokyo, Takamiya 6
LJ II.1, now Chicago, Newberry 32.9
LJ II.8, now San Marino, Huntington HM 26054

Hereford, Cathedral Lib.
O.3.5: 67.5/1, 673.5/1, 1134.5/1, 1220/2, 1429.5/1, 3743.6/1, 3973.5/1, 4049.7/1, 4049.8/1, 4263.6/1
O.4.14: 542/1, 620/3, 770/1, 1071/1, 1139/4, 3520/2, 3570/1, 3712/2, 4129/6
P.1.9: 2017.5/22, 4056/21
P.7.7: 4150/24

Hertford, County Record Office
15857A (no number in *IMEV*): 3632/33

Holkham Hall, Earl of Leicester
667: 4019/48
668: 1193/4
670: 979/14

Hopton Hall
Sotheby Dec 1989, now Quaritch: 1786/3

Huddersfield, West Yorks Archive Service
DD/R/dd/V/30 (Ramsden rental): 2224.5/2

Ipswich County Hall, Hillwood, now New Haven, Yale, Beinecke 365

Ipswich, Public Lib.
6 (kept at Ipswich School): 1820/8

Ipswich, Suffolk Record Office
Ipswich Great Doomsday: 3632/34

Kilkenny Castle, now Dublin, National Lib. of Ireland, D 1435

Kilkenny Corporation Archives
Liber primus Kilkenniensis: 3634.1/1

Kilkenny, St Canice's Lib.
Red Book of Ossory: 684/1, 891/1, 1120.5/1, 1123/1, 1214.4/1, 1265/1, 2037.5/1

Kraus Cat.22, no. 21, now Boston Public Lib. 1527

Leeds, Univ. Lib.
Brotherton 500: 3428/75
Brotherton 501: 621.5/11, 879.5/11, 2725/2, 3266/13, 3389/20, 3397/13, 3428/77 = also 3428/89, 4110.5/11

Leeds, Yorks Archaeological Soc.
DD 121/109 (on deposit from Appleby Castle): 595/21

Leicester, Old Town Hall Lib.
4: 173.5/1, 782.8/1, 1963.5/1, 4128.5/1

Leiden Univ. Lib.
Vossius Germ.Gall.Q 9 (Vossius 9 in *IMEV*): 36/4, 658/11, 809/18, 824/42, 875/5, 1168/20*, 1300/2, 1481/7, 1582/1, 1875/6, 2000.3/1, 2201/1, 2233/22, 2464/13, 2590/6, 2606/4, 2625/10, 2784/14, 2825/6, 3197/2, 3502/6, 3632/38, 3661/10, 3844.5/1, 4112/7, 4131/1, 4196/1

Lichfield, Cathedral Lib.
16 (6 in *IMEV*): 3429/13
18 (no number in *IMEV*): 4017/9
29 (2 in *IMEV*): 1913/23, 4019/42
50 (18 in *IMEV*): 3429/14

Lincoln, Cathedral Lib.
44: 142/A8, 142/B12, 191/7, 495/6, 498/11, 565/9, 594/8, 798/8, 1003/12, 1127/8, 1141/9, 1150/9, 1204/11, 1223/9, 1321/6, 1822/9, 1935/10, 2001/A9, 2001/B9, 2002/9, 2058/8, 2077/7, 2114/9, 2283/7, 2298/10, 2329/12, 2596/7, 2729/7, 2775/10, 2832/7, 3081/10, 3133/8, 3147/7, 3254/9, 3273/9, 3275/9, 3281/8, 3282/10, 3287/10, 3339/9, 3350/8, 3408/10, 3463/8, 3649/6, 3716/7, 3802/9, 3863/12, 4035/6, 4134/6, 4143/9, 4151/9, 4156/6, 4239/7
66: 4277/1
91 (Thornton): 11/2, 172/6, 229/2, 246/1, 365/6, 406/A10, 704/12,

(continued overleaf)

Lincoln, Cathedral Lib.

775/3, 1184/9, 1292/1, 1566/3, 1674/1, 1681/4, 1692/1, 1722/1, 1725/6, 1741/1, 1757/2, 1781/14, 1853/1, 1918/2, 1950.5/2, 1953/2, 1954/1, 1990/1, 2026/1, 2099/2, 2322/1, 2608/1, 2616/1, 3428/F, 3709/1, 3730/2, 3921/2

100: 3169/1

103: 1597/18

105: 2371/1

110: 4019/43

129: 1875/5, 2590/5, 2784/10, 2806/1, 3748/4

132: 2830.5/1, 3895/1

133: 1305/1

189: 430.5/5

234: 141.5/1, 594/10

Littledale, now Oxford, Bodleian, Don.e.120

Liverpool, Cathedral

6, kept in Univ. Lib. (from Quaritch Cat. 1931, item 73): 735.5/1

Liverpool, Univ. Lib.

F.4.8: 1459/A12

F.4.9: 245/35 **(no number in *IMEV*)**, 3507/8

London, British Lib.

Add.2283: 4226/4

Add.4900: 2255.6/1

Add.5140: 3928/15, 4019/10

Add.5464: 3750/1

Add.5465: 0.2/1, 1/1, 13/1, 146.5/1, 155.5/1, 364/1, 456.5/1, 490.5/1, 497/2, 506.5/1, 557.5/1, 649.5/1, 675.8/1, 1273.3/1, 1327/1, 1328.5/1, 1339.5/1, 1450/1, 1636.5/1, 1731/1, 1866.8/1, 1999.5/1, 2007.5/1, 2028.8/1, 2200.3/1, 2277/1, 2364/5, 2394.5/1, 2530.5/1, 2547.5/1, 2832.2/1, 3131/1, 3162.5/1, 3193.5/3, 3206.5/1, 3270.5/1, 3297.3/1, 3297.5/1, 3437/5, 3597/2, 3724.5/1, 3751.3/1, 3845/12, 3903.8/1, 4098.6/1, 4184/11, 4281.5/1

Add.5467: 42.3/1, 1955.5/3, 2233/20

Add.5665: 18/3, 31/1, 54.5/1, 113.5/1, 263.5/1, 263.8/1, 474.5/1, 507/1, 581/1, 680/1, 681/1, 753.8/1, 887/1, 918/1, 962/1, 1212/1, 1214.5/1, 1234/3, 1303.3/1, 1315/1, 1322/1, 1578/1, 1589.5/2, 1710/1, 1738/1, 2044/1, 2053/4, 2244.6/1, 2277.5/1, 2323.8/1, 2370/1, 2377/2, 2388/1, 2393.5/1, 2409/1, 2453/1, 2533/1, 2636/1, 2731/1, 2737.5/1, 3168.4/1, 3315/1, 3318.4/4, 3376.5/1, 3382/1, 3652/1, 3677.5/1, 3737/1, 3776/5, 3832.5/2, 3950/1, 3975/2, 3988/1, 4077/1, 4283.5/1

Add.5666: 1352/1, 2323.3/1, 3595/1, 3596/3

Add.5901: 968/2a

Add.6159: 2698/8, 4113/12

Add.6702: 365/e, 4148/15

Add.8151: 190/3, 245/26, 906/9, 1920/5, 3274/2, 4006/2

Add.9066: 849.5/1, 860.5/1, 906/10, 1391.8/1, 2238.5/3, 3322.3/3, 3818.5/1, 4074.5/1

Add.9832: 100/A8

Add.10036: 1881/7, 2157/4, 2165/5

Add.10052: 1342/25, 1491/15, 2119/22, 2167/28, 4150/22

Add.10053: 244/6, 2320/C7

Add.10099: 824/30, 4112/5

Add.10106: 4175/2

Add.10301: 56/11, 57/10, 58/10, 59/11, 82/16, 791/17, 1788/9, 1859/18, 1911/17, 2127/11, 2304/13, 2839/16, 2842/15, 2843/16, 2844/17, 2850/17, 2854/19, 2856/15, 2858/13, 2860/16, 2866/17, 2868/14, 2872/14, 2874/12, 2876/14, 2878/15, 2880/18, 2884/19, 2889/15, 2895/13, 2905/19, 2906/12, 2910/17, 2912/14, 2918/15, 2945/17, 2949/17, 2950/18, 2951/15, 2956/11, 2957/15, 2960/11, 2987/16, 2989/17, 2990/19, 2991/14, 2991/4, 2994/15, 3004/17, 3017/13, 3026/16, 3029/A12, 3035/15, 3036/11, 3037/17, 3041/15, 3042/14, 3048/18, 3051/15, 3052/15, 3060/11, 3066/15, 3067/17, 3068/18, 3266/12, 3384/11, 3388/16, 3389/18, 3813/15, 4266/16

Add.10302: 3772/19

Add.10303: 923/1, 3947/1

Add.10304: 2642/1

Add.10305: 716/7

Add.10336: 3615/1, 3765.5/1

Add.10340: 809/13, 4019/58

Add.10392: 3656.5/1

Add.10574: 1459/B14

Add.10626: 2837/3, 2891/5, 2894/12, 3035/16, 3452/8, 3997/4

Add.11304: 3428/48

Add.11305: 3429/11

Add.11306: 1961/6

Add.11307: 373/3a, 824/31, 1034/1, 1261/1, 1718/8, 1869/6

Add.11579: 1366/1, 1415.5/1, 1863.8/1, 2051/1, 2093/2, 2328/1, 3078/2, 3513/3, 3701/1, 4088/4
Add.11748: 2577/7
Add.11814: 1526/1
Add.12043: 2662/B4
Add.12044: 3327/13
Add.12195: 199/12, 1137.3/1, 1636.3/1
Add.12524: 100/A7, 4082/2
Add.14408: 935/15, 4194.5/1
Add.14848: 1513/1
Add.14866: 2514/1
Add.14997: 1608/2, 2343/1, 2683/1
Add.15225: 3992/1
Add.15233: 782.5/1, 2668.8/1
Add.15237: 750/4, 1342/26, 2119/23, 2167/29, 3687/11, 4150/23
Add.15549: 3616/1
Add.16165: 147/3, 650/1, 746/3, 837.5/1, 851/7, 886/1, 1288/1, 1426/1, 1496/1, 1507/7, 1635/2, 2060/2, 2571/1, 2611/1, 3256/1, 3437/6, 3504/4, 3656/5, 3670/7, 3671/2, 3914/3
Add.16170: 2320/B13
Add.17011: 1496.5/1
Add.17012: 2030.6/1
Add.17013: 1436.5/1, 3084.3/1
Add.17102: 2030.8/1
Add.17376: 1495/1, 2107/1, 2226/1, 3107/1, 3199/1, 3417/1, 3681/1
Add.17492: 13.8/2, 232/1, 666/11, 813.6/1, 848.5/1, 1086/7, 1270.2/1, 1409.3/1, 1418.5/1, 1609.5/1, 2281.5/1, 2577.5/1, 3174.5/1, 3670/9, 3909.6/1, 4201.6/1, 4217.6/1, **(3914.5, not in *IMEV*)**
Add.17866: 1408/2, 2627/11, 4094.5/1
Add.18216: 3848/21
Add.18631: 727/A4
Add.18632: 2229/35, 3928/16
Add.18752: 681.5/1 **(Add.18652 in *SUP*)**, 813.6/2, 1356.8/1, 1414.8/1, 1864.5/2, (2195.5/1 = next), 2224.5/1, 2245.3/1, 2245.6/1, 2249/2, 2255.6/2, 2307.5/1, 2619.5/1, 2736.6/1, 2736.8/1, 2753.5/1, 3880.6/1
Add.19046: 3742/1
Add.19252: 2574/26
Add.19452: 2574/27
Add.19674: 1293/5
Add.19677: 727/A5, 1105/C4
Add.19901: 1728/4
Add.20059: 181/1, 452/1, 651/1, 1528.5/1, 2546/1, 3364/1, 3391/1
Add.20091: 1078/1a, 2025/1a, 3754/7a, 4146/1a
Add.20775: 4082/2a
Add.21202: 1286/6, 1342/27, 1491/16, 2119/24, 2167/30
Add.21253: 1281/1
Add.21410: 1168/15, 2523/2
Add.22029: 2577/8
Add.22121: 1286/7, 1342/28, 1491/17, 2119/25, 2167/31
Add.22139: 809/14, 2662/A18, 3190/9, 3348/9, 3787/7
Add.22283: 5/2, 25/9, 40/6, 79/6, 188/2, 197.8/5, 220/11, 245/27, 247/2, 286/7, 291/6, 351/5, 374/3, 395/2, 414/2, 419/2, 485/6, 562/6, 563/3, 583/2, 606/2, 678/2, 820/2, 872/2, 937/2, 974/2, 975/3, 1081/2, 1090/2, 1095/2, 1099/2, 1102/2, 1108/2, 1109/2, 1117/4, 1118/5, 1136/5, 1144/4, 1367.5/5, 1369/1, 1379/4, 1402/2, 1443/2, 1448/2, 1455/2, 1462/2, 1464/7, 1469/4, 1476/2, 1482/9, 1512/2, 1521/5, 1532/2, 1537/2, 1596/2, 1643/8, 1646/6, 1647/6, 1648/5, 1657/5, 1684/3, 1695/2, 1696/2, 1712/2, 1745/2, 1763/2, 1765/2, 1783/2, 1784/2, 1887/2, 1898/2, 1959/2, 1962/2, 1969/3, 2017.5/20, 2020/2, 2094/6, 2108/2, 2250/7, 2270/6, 2280/2, 2302/2, 2320/C8, 2605/3, 2607/2, 2718/2, 2720/2, 2780/8, 2790/2, 2859/4, 2907/4, 2928/2, 2935/4, 2937/6, 2940/4, 2944/2, 2965/3, 2969/3, 2972/2, 2976/5, 2978/4, 3002/5, 3003/6, 3009/5, 3020/5, 3105/2, 3238/4, 3247/2, 3270/3, 3316/2, 3326/2, 3419/2, 3420/3, 3428/49, 3453/5, 3501/3, 3553/3, 3590/5, 3591/5, 3663/2, 3683/5, 3708/5, 3738/5, 3739/5, 3760/2, 3791/5, 3816/8, 3826/3, 3829/4, 3833/2, 3839/2, 3841/2, 3842/2, 3925/2, 3952/2, 3996/2, 4056/18, 4135/1, 4157/2, 4158/2, 4250/5, 4268/2
Add.22504: 3265.5/1
Add.22558: 245/28
Add.22577: 260/1a
Add.22718: 994.5/1, 1333/2, 2090/3
Add.22720: 579/2, 3088/3
Add.23198: 4149/1a
Add.23986: 668/1
Add.24078: 907/11, 2932/20
Add.24194: 399.5/5, 746.5/5, 1426.6/5, 1637.6/5, 2361.5/5, 2736.2/5, 2831.4/5, 3218.3/5, 4189.5/5

(continued overleaf)

(continued overleaf)

1961.3/1, 2034/1, 2070/3, 2331/1, 3238.5/1, 3578.5/1, 3579/1, 3762/1
Arundel 59: 935/9, 2229/22
Arundel 83: 1270/1
Arundel 99: 2516/11
Arundel 119: 3928/11
Arundel 140: 220/8, 1101/4, 3187/A3, 3429/5
Arundel 168: 6/3, 576/3, 607/1, 824/15, 854/11, 2447/2, 2574/15, 2877/1, 3955/7
Arundel 220: 1851/1, 2691.8/1
Arundel 231 (2): 1085/1
Arundel 248: 888/1, 1697/1, 3432/1, 4223/3
Arundel 249: 2154/1
Arundel 272: 3422/5
Arundel 285: 276.5/2, 648/1, 1040/1, 1044/1, 1070.3/1, 1077/1, 1119/1, 1343/1, 1703/6, 1727/8, 2161.5/2, 2464/5, 2486/1, 2528/1, 2551.5/1, 3243/1, 3584/1, 3695/1, 3776.5/2, 3777.5/1, 3904/1
Arundel 286: 1787/1, 3823.5/1
Arundel 288: 2320/A9
Arundel 292: 787/1, 1326/1, 1422/1, 1952/1, 2100/1, 3227/1, 3413/1, 3819/1, 3969/4
Arundel 327: 347/1, 589/1, 1414/1, 1812/1, 2019/1, 2621/1, 2651/1, 2849/1, 3508/1, 3509/1, 3817/1, 3936/1, 4073/1, 4086/1
Arundel 359: 4244.5/1
Arundel 396: 6/4, 4246/7
Arundel 507: 406/A7, 1343/2, 3110/1, 3568/4, 4031/1
Cotton App.VII: 1879/1, 3428/40
Cotton App.VIII: 2574/16
Cotton App.XXVII: 447/5, 3928/12
Cotton Augustus A.IV: 2516/12
Cotton Caligula A.II: 83/1, 220/9, 256/2, 272/1, 562/4, 563/2, 567/1, 824/16, 931/2, 951/2, 982/1, 1046/2, 1172/1, 1184/6, 1355/1, 1511/2, 1583/3, 1690/2, 1701/3, 1724/2, 1725/3, 1766/1, 1774/1, 1823/3, 2233/14, 2411/1, 2784/6, 2894/8, 2922/9, 3225/1, 3345/1, 3371/1, 3553/2, 3836/1, 3845/9, 4153/1, 4154/5
Cotton Caligula A.IX: 295/1, 1091/2, 1384/2, 2070/4, 2687/3, 3517/4, 3967/4, 4016/1, 4051/2
Cotton Caligula A.XI: 727/A1, 1105/C3 **(Caligula A.IX in *IMEV*), 1459/B12**
Cotton Charters.IV 18: 3300/4
Cotton Claudius A.II: 462/5, 956.5/1, 961/6, 3372/1, 4068.3/5
Cotton Claudius D.VII: 4174/1
Cotton Cleopatra B.II: 2663/1, 2777/1
Cotton Cleopatra B.VI: 519/1, 1062/3, 2037/1, 2706/1
Cotton Cleopatra C.IV: 734.8/3, 1620/1, 3213/1, 3308.5/2, 3799/1, 4008/C13, 4025/1
Cotton Cleopatra C.VI: 734.5/1, 1820/5, 1917/2, 2285/1, 3568/5
Cotton Cleopatra D.VI: 3122/4
Cotton Cleopatra D.VII: 809/10, 2029/2, 3190/6, 3348/5
Cotton Cleopatra D.VIII: 91/2, 3280/3, 3970/2
Cotton Cleopatra D.IX: 50/6, 56/7, 57/7, 58/7, 59/7, 204/1, 907/7, 1788/6, 2873/8, 2932/14, 3064/7, 3266/8
Cotton Cleopatra F.III: 557/1
Cotton Domitianus.XVIII: 306.8/1
Cotton Faustina A.V: 3665.3/1, 3859.5/1
Cotton Faustina B.III: 243/1, 3090/1
Cotton Faustina B.VI: 86.8/1, 91.8/1, 672/1, 2463/1
Cotton Faustina B.VII: 1387/1
Cotton Faustina C.XII: 954/1
Cotton Galba A.XIX: 433/1
Cotton Galba E.VIII: 979/5, 2039.3/2, 3558.5/2, 3632/19
Cotton Galba E.IX: 189/1, 259/1, 512/1, 585/1, 694/3, 709/1, 788/2, 987/1, 110/3, 1112/1, 1146/1, 1176/1, 1401/1, 1480/2, 1497/1, 2080/3, 2149/1, 2189/1, 3080/1, 3117/1, 3187/C2, 3428/39, 3796/1, 3801/1, 3899/1, 3912.5/1
Cotton Julius A.V: 310/A3, 313/A3, 368/1, 379/1, 814/4, 841/4, 2686/A3, 2754/A4, 3352/4
Cotton Julius B.I: 1929/2, 4198.8/1
Cotton Julius B.II: 3799/2
Cotton Julius B.XII: 1186/2, 2199.5/1, 2200.5/1, 2212.5/1, 2214/2, 2215/2, 2216/2, 3884.5/1, 3885.5/1
Cotton Julius D.VIII: 444/6
Cotton Julius D.IX: 50/7, 56/8, 58/8, 59/8, 82/10, 184/9, 201/9, 721/10, 791/13, 907/14, 1859/13, 1911/12, 2304/11, 2839/12, 2841/3, 2843/11, 2844/12, 2845/6, 2848/9, 2850/13, 2854/14, 2856/10, 2858/10, 2860/11, 2862/5, 2866/13, 2868/11, 2870/7, 2872/10, 2873/9, 2874/10, 2875/12, 2876/10, 2878/11, 2880/14, 2882/9, 2884/14,

2886/10, 2887/9, 2888/3, 2889/12, 2891/2, 2894/9, 2895/10, 2897/6, 2899/7, 2900/5, 2905/14, 2906/9, 2910/13, 2911/3, 2912/11, 2914/1, 2915/7, 2916/2, 2918/11, 2922/15, 2932/15, 2945/11, 2949/12, 2950/13, 2951/11, 2953/5, 2954/11, 2957/11, 2958/7, 2959/8, 2961/11, 2973/8, 2987/11, 2989/13, 2990/13, 2991/10, 2994/9, 3004/12, 3005/10, 3017/9, 3026/12, 3029/A7, 3033/12, 3035/11, 3037/13, 3041/11, 3042/10, 3046/10, 3048/13, 3050/8, 3051/10, 3052/11, 3053/3, 3055/10, 3059/13, 3063/12, 3064/15, 3066/11, 3067/13, 3068/15, 3091/6, 3266/9, 3384/8, 3388/10, 3389/12, 3813/12, 4266/13

Cotton Julius E.IV: 444/7

Cotton Julius F.X: 1295/1

Cotton Nero A.VI: 3444/4, 3929/1

Cotton Nero A.X: 635/1, 2262.5/1 **(A.IX in *SUP*)**, 2739/1, 2744/1, 3144/1

Cotton Nero A.XIV: 631/1, 734.5/2, 3568/6

Cotton Nero C.XII: 1219.5/1

Cotton Nero D.V: 2988/6

Cotton Nero D.XI: 399/1, 1377/1

Cotton Otho A.XVIII, burned, Transcript at Cat.643, M.4: 3190/14, 3327/K, 3787/11

Cotton Otho B.V: 2988/7

Cotton Otho C.XIII: 295/2

Cotton Rolls II 23: 544/1, 818/1, 1138/1, 2338/1, 2834.3/1, 3451.5/1, 3455/1, 4018/2, 4029/4, 4261/1

Cotton Tiberius A.VII: 4265/1

Cotton Tiberius B.III: 914/2

Cotton Tiberius B.XIII: 1940.5/1

Cotton Tiberius D.VII: 399.5/2, 746.5/2, 1426.6/2, 1637.6/2, 2736.2/2, 2831.4/2, 3218.3/2, 4189.5/2

Cotton Tiberius D.VIII: 2361.5/2

Cotton Tiberius E.II: 3519/1

Cotton Tiberius E.VII: 25/6, 26/6, 32/6, 46/4, 47/6, 53/1, 75/1, 85/1, 128/1, 170/2, 198/1, 245/20, 287/1, 288/3, 289/7, 314/6, 316/1, 319/1, 330/1, 331/1, 332/1, 386/1, 387/1, 388/1, 389/1, 390/1, 391/1, 392/1, 393/1, 394/1, 539/3, 599/1, 626/1, 627/1, 677/1, 713/1, 771/2, 807/1, 863/1, 876/1, 948/1, 1442/1, 1482/6, 1493/1, 1516/1, 1519/5, 1520/1, 1547/1, 1572/1, 1573/1, 1584/1, 1612/1, 1616/1, 1623/1, 1643/5, 1645/4, 1660/1, 1668/1, 1670/1, 1671/1, 1689/1, 1698/1, 1716/1, 1773/1, 1792/1, 1800/1, 2022/1, 2033.3/1, 2144/1, 2638/1, 2713/1, 2722/1, 2723/1, 2847/1, 2857/1, 2869/1, 2917/1, 2920/1, 2925/1, 2931/1, 2936/5, 2938/4, 2939/4, 2943/1, 2946/1, 2947/1, 2948/1, 2964/1, 2966/1, 2967/3, 2970/4, 2971/5, 2975/1, 2979/1, 2980/1, 2981/1, 2982/1, 2983/1, 2984/1, 2985/1, 2986/1, 2997/1, 2998/1, 3000/1, 3001/1, 3003/5, 3004.5/1, 3006/1, 3007/1, 3010/1, 3011/1, 3014/1, 3016/1, 3018/5, 3022/1, 3023/1, 3024/1, 3025/1, 3028/2, 3032/1, 3044/1, 3045/1, 3047/1, 3054/1, 3062/1, 3166/1, 3167/1, 3176/1, 3177/1, 3178/1, 3392/1, 3394/1, 3425/1, 3516/1, 3548/1, 3592/6, 3617/1, 3758/1, 3816/6, 3830/1, 3840/1, 3865/5, 3933/5, 3934/1, 3935/1, 3941/1, 3953/1, 3974/1, 3977/1, 3978/1, 3979/1, 3981/1, 3982/1, 3984/1, 4002/1, 4032/1, 4048/1, 4049/1, 4250/3

Cotton Titus A.XX: 1445.6/3

Cotton Titus A.XXIII: 3185/3

Cotton Titus A.XXV: 1507.5/1

Cotton Titus A.XXVI: 216/1, 220/10, 533/2, 704/10, 957/1, 1297/9, 1998/4, 2358.5/1b, 2487/1, 2950/20, 3091/9

Cotton Titus C.XIX: 302/3, 4160/10

Cotton Titus D.XI: 2794.2/2

Cotton Titus D.XII: 3815.8/1

Cotton Titus D.XVIII: 3568/7

Cotton Titus D.XX: 824/48, 3632/20

Cotton Vespasian A.III: 483/10, 694/4, 780/2, 788/3, 959/2, 1775/2, 1786/1, 1885/2, 2153/4, 2685/2, 3208/2, 3976/4

Cotton Vespasian A.XII: 3193.5/2, 3862.5/1

Cotton Vespasian A.XXV: 102.3/1, 218/1, 933/1, 1727/9, 2590/3

Cotton.Vespasian B.XII: 202/1

Cotton Vespasian B.XVI: 1459/C10, 1555/1, 1926/1, 3929/2, 3973/6

Cotton Vespasian D.VII: 3103/4

Cotton Vespasian D.VIII: 2321/2

Cotton Vespasian D.IX: 316.3/1, 751/1, 1172/2, 1907/9, 2308.8/1, 2491/1

Cotton Vespasian D.XIII: 2186/1

Cotton Vespasian E.VIII: 4008/B11

Cotton Vespasian E.XVI: 1583/4

Cotton Vitellius A.I: 688/5

(continued overleaf)

London, British Lib.

Cotton Vitellius A.XVI: 671.5/1, 1270.4/1, 1273.8/1, 1322.8/1, 1637.4/1, 1933.5/2, 2028.3/1, 2030.2/1, 2030.4/1, 3704.6/1, 3706.3/1, 3810.6/1, 3880.3/1, 4095.5/1
Cotton Vitellius C.XIII: 4265/2
Cotton Vitellius D.III: 2288.8/2
Cotton Vitellius D.XI: 2358.5/1a
Cotton Vitellius D.XII: 969/2
Cotton Vitellius D.XX, burned in 1731: 1608.5/1
Cotton Vitellius E.X: 365/3, 729.5/1, 3491/9
Cotton Vitellius F.XIII: 3458.5/1, 3473.5/1
Egerton 613: 1272/5, 1407/1, 1923/1, 2645/2, 3221/1
Egerton 614: 3103/5
Egerton 615: 233/5, 263/5, 540/4, 1242/5, 1243/5, 1244/5, 1245/5, 1246/5, 1247/5, 1248/5, 1249/5, 1296/5, 1719/5, 2428/5
Egerton 657: 3428/41
Egerton 833: 624/3, 4035/15
Egerton 845: 3253/1, 3452.5/1, 3528/1
Egerton 913: 2662/A13
Egerton 927: 4145/1
Egerton 1151: 302/4
Egerton 1624: 362/1, 1190/1
Egerton 1991: 2662/A14
Egerton 1992: 710/6
Egerton 1993: 38/4, 82/11, 213/A1, 574/2, 791/14, 907/8, 1859/14, 1911/13, 2127/8, 2304/12, 2632/4, 2643/1, 2717/3, 2838/3, 2839/13, 2841/4, 2842/10, 2843/12, 2844/13, 2848/10, 2850/14, 2854/15, 2856/11, 2858/11, 2860/12, 2866/14, 2867/4, 2872/11, 2876/11, 2878/12, 2880/15, 2883/5, 2884/15, 2885/3, 2891/3, 2895/11, 2899/8, 2905/15, 2906/10, 2910/14, 2912/12, 2915/8, 2918/12, 2922/10, 2932/16, 2945/12, 2949/13, 2950/14, 2951/12, 2953/6, 2956/9, 2957/12, 2958/8, 2960/9, 2961/12, 2987/12, 2989/14, 2990/14, 2991/11, 2994/10, 3004/13, 3017/10, 3026/13, 3029/A8, 3030/3, 3033/13, 3035/12, 3036/9, 3037/14, 3041/12, 3042/11, 3046/11, 3048/14, 3049/3, 3051/11, 3052/12, 3059/14, 3060/9, 3063/13, 3066/12, 3067/14, 3068/16, 3091/7, 3384/9, 3388/11, 3389/13, 3704.3/1, 3813/13, 3973/7, 4266/14
Egerton 1995: 317/4, 824/17, 979/6, 1014.5/1, 1147.9/1, 1152.5/1, 1240.5/1, 1920/3, 1929/5, 3187/A4, 3546/1, 3632/21, 3848/11, 3985/4
Egerton 2257: 704/12a, 979/8a, 1116/1a, 1288/1a, 1292/1a, 1497/1a, 1722/1a, 1871/1a, 3435/1a, 3553/2a, 3709/1a, 3921/1a, 4153/1a
Egerton 2572: 3848/12
Egerton 2642: 2451.5/1
Egerton 2711: 13.8/1
Egerton 2726: 1913/13, 4019/32
Egerton 2788: 2145/4, 4042.5/1, 4181/14
Egerton 2810: 82/12, 184/10, 201/10, 256/3, 791/15, 907/9, 1530/1, 1859/15, 1911/14, 2671/1, 2839/14, 2842/11, 2843/13, 2844/14, 2848/11, 2850/15, 2854/16, 2856/12, 2860/13, 2866/15, 2870/8, 2872/12, 2873/10, 2875/13, 2880/16 = also 2880/21 **(olim Allan of Darlington)**, 2884/16, 2886/11, 2887/10, 2889/13, 2894/10, 2895/12, 2905/16, 2910/15, 2912/13, 2916/3, 2932/17, 2945/13, 2949/14, 2950/15, 2951/13, 2954/12, 2959/9, 2961/13, 2973/9, 2987/13, 2989/15, 2990/15, 2994/11, 3004/14, 3005/11, 3026/14, 3033/14, 3035/13, 3037/15, 3041/13, 3046/12, 3048/15, 3052/13, 3053/4, 3055/11, 3059/15, 3061/1, 3063/14, 3064/8, 3066/13, 3067/15, 3068/17, 3335/1, 3336/1, 3337/1, 3338/1, 3380//2, 3384/10, 3388/12, 3389/14, 3453/4, 3813/14, 4266/15
Egerton 2862: 1895/4, 1979/3, 1993/A3, 2288.8/3, 3139/1
Egerton 2863: 1913/14, 4019/33
Egerton 2864: 3928/13, 4019/5
Egerton 2891: 50/8, 56/9, 57/8, 59/9, 82/13, 184/11, 201/11, 273/7, 409/7, 483/11, 578/6, 719/6, 721/11, 1546/11, 1788/7, 1809/10, 1859/16, 1911/15, 2105/5, 2106/7, 2120/8, 2127/9, 2647/9, 2755/11, 2839/15, 2842/12, 2843/14, 2844/15, 2848/12, 2850/16, 2854/17, 2856/13, 2860/14, 2866/16, 2868/12, 2870/9, 2872/13, 2874/11, 2875/14, 2876/12, 2878/13, 2880/17, 2882/10, 2884/17, 2886/12, 2889/14, 2897/7, 2899/9, 2905/17, 2910/16, 2918/13, 2922/11, 2945/14, 2949/15, 2950/16,

2951/14, 2954/13, 2957/13, 2958/9, 2959/10, 2960/10, 2973/10, 2987/14, 2990/16, 2991/12, 2994/12, 3004/15, 3005/12, 3017/11, 3026/15, 3029/A9, 3033/15, 3035/14, 3036/10, 3037/16, 3042/12, 3046/13, 3048/16, 3050/9, 3051/12, 3052/14, 3055/12, 3066/14, 3067/16, 3091/8, 3266/10, 3388/13, 3389/15, 3664/8, 3766/7, 3767/7

Egerton 3002: 1589.5/1

Egerton 3143: 261/1, 1038.5/1, 1048.8/1, 1078.5/1, 3677/1

Egerton 3245 (*IMEV* gives several entries as 'olim Gurney'): 196.5/1, 197.8/8, 246/2, 271/1, 790/1, 981/4, 1197.1/1, 1367.5/10, 1368/1, 1691/1, 1729/3, 1761/8, 1781/16, 1950.5/1, 1951/1, 2017.5/25, 2035/1, 2096/1, 2250/10, 2270/9, 3428/70, 3557/1, 3769.8/1, 3882/1, 4056/24

Egerton 3307: 187.5/1, 340/3, 772.5/1, 1030.5/1, 1070.5/1, 1220.5/1, 1234/4, 1363.5/1, 1651.5/1, 2674.5/1, 3674/2, 4229.5/1

Egerton 3309: 1185/1, 2879/1, 4067/1

Egerton 3425: 615/1

Greenville 35 (not identified, this is not printed book Grenville 35): 3407/1b

Harley 43: 854/12, 1597/13, 3405.8/1

Harley 44: 1597/14

Harley 45: 1410/1, 2303/1, 2549/1

Harley 51: 3844/1

Harley 63: 1703/15

Harley 78: 186/3, 444/8, 663/3, 1379/3, 2364/6, 2441/1, 2756/6, 3414/1, 3491/12, 3491/13, 3491/4

Harley 114: 310/A10, 313/A10, 814/13, 841/13, 2686/A13, 2754/A13, 3352/13

Harley 116: 68/1, 576/4, 654/3, 854/13, 951/3, 1139/1, 1147.4/1, 1149/1, 1297/3, 1400/2, 1418/1, 2136/1, 2229/23, 2411/2, 2591/5, 2784/7, 3088/1, 3955/8, 4184/6, 4230/4

Harley 153: 598/2, 2988/8

Harley 165: 4258.6/3

Harley 172: 199/5, 512.5/1, 854/14, 1168/10*, 1540/6, 3121/4

Harley 201: 727/A3

Harley 206: 1342/18, 1491/12, 2119/16, 2167/19, 4150/15

Harley 210: 462/6, 3027/3, 3231/4, 3241/4

Harley 211: 621.5/6, 879.5/6, 1758.5/1, 4110.5/6

Harley 215: 1907/10

Harley 218: 646/1, 1464.5/1, 2464/6

Harley 219: 3513/2

Harley 226: 979/7

Harley 237: 4184/7

Harley 245: 2462.5/1

Harley 247: 1941.8/1, 3440/6

Harley 271: 854/15, 3491/14, 3955/9

Harley 275: 340/1

Harley 293: 1620/2, 2547.3/1

Harley 322: 2988/9

Harley 364: 3444/7

Harley 367: 439/4, 582/2, 595/15, 746/2, 928/5, 981.3/1, 1168/11*, 2264/4, 2445/6, 2547.3/2, 3154.5/1, 3759/1

Harley 372: 86/1, 530/5, 537/1, 882/1, 928/6, 1086/4, 1804/1, 1934/4, 2081/4, 2229/24, 2445/7, 2556/4, 3440/7, 3670/5, 4254.5/3, 4255/1

Harley 435: 245/21

Harley 485: 1427.5/1, 3712/1, 3871/1

Harley 486: 3372.8/1

Harley 494: 1703/16

Harley 525: 1101/5, 2780/6, 3139/2

Harley 533: 1608.5/2a

Harley 536: 1464.5/2, 3113/2

Harley 541: 549/2, 824/18, 995.4/1, 1920/4, 2333/1, 2412.5/1, 4155/3, 4181/6, 4209/1

Harley 542: 2200/1, 3759/2

Harley 545: 941/2

Harley 559: 365/d, 734.8/4, 1112/3, 3308.5/3, 4008/Aa, 4018/3, 4029/5

Harley 565: 969/3, 3799/3, 4198.8/2

Harley 614: 33/3

Harley 629: 2574/17, 2742/7

Harley 661: 710/7

Harley 665: 475.8/2, 513/3, 616/1, 744/1, 1207/1, 2757/1, 2789/2, 3079.8/1, 3209.5/1, 3753/1

Harley 667: 2993/1

Harley 671: 752.5/1

Harley 682: 3/1, 9/1, 15/1, 62/1, 84/1, 129/1, 133/1, 136/1, 140/1, 144/1, 148/1, 151/1, 157/1, 164/1, 165/1, 175/1, 238/1, 264/1, 300/1, 309/1, 329/1, 335/1, 336/1, 337/1,

(continued overleaf)

338/1, 382/1, 403/2, 431/1, 440/1, 451/1, 460/1, 472/1, 510/1, 517/1, 552/1, 553/1, 555/1 **(Harley 692 in *IMEV*),** 570/1, 571/1, 647/1, 656/1, 682/1, 764/1, 810/1, 816/1, 827/1, 833/1, 852/1, 857/1, 867/1, 924/1, 960/1, 1022/1, 1023/1, 1088/1, 1239/1, 1240/1, 1250/1, 1256/1, 1257/1, 1313/1, 1316/1, 1339/1, 1345/1, 1385/1, 1403/1, 1404/1, 1413/1, 1420/1, 1424/1, 1500/1, 1529/1, 1549/1, 1581/1, 1607/1, 1628/1, 1858/1, 1933/1, 2027/1, 2028/1, 2030/1, 2032/1, 2175/1, 2177/1, 2180/1, 2181/1, 2184/1, 2196/1, 2197/1, 2198/2, 2203/1, 2204/1, 2205/1, 2206/1, 2243/1, 2259/1, 2261/1, 2265/1, 2266/1, 2274/1, 2275/1, 2276/1, 2278/1, 2294/1, 2299/1, 2300/1, 2308/1, 2309/1, 2325.5/1, 2358/1, 2378/1, 2379/1, 2406/1, 2422/1, 2423/1, 2424.5/1, 2424/1, 2425/1, 2427/1, 2436/1, 2438/1, 2439/1, 2449/1, 2450/1, 2455/1, 2456/1, 2457/2, 2458/1, 2482/1, 2548/1, 2550/1, 2558/1, 2564/1, 2581/1, 2602.2/1, 2623/1, 2648/1, 2669/1, 2699/1, 2758/1, 2768/1, 2798/1, 2813/1, 2819/1, 2827/1, 2828/1, 3099/1, 3124/1, 3128/1, 3132/1, 3134/1, 3140/1, 3141/1, 3142/1, 3163/1, 3181/1, 3229/1, 3255/1, 3360/1, 3370/1, 3396/1, 3426/1, 3439/1, 3447/1, 3458/1, 3465/1, 3541/1, 3586/1, 3601/1, 3622/1, 3626/1, 3631/1, 3633/1, 3645/1, 3688/1, 3702/1, 3723/1, 3768/1, 3794/1, 3795/1, 3875/1, 3885/1, 3890/1, 3897/1, 3912/1, 3916/1, 3949/1, 3956/1, 3960/1, 3962/1, 3972/1, 3995/1, 4024/1, 4027/1, 4069/1, 4120/2, 4161/1, 4188/1, 4191/1, 4192/1, 4195/1, 4213/1, 4242/1, 4283/1, 4284/1

Harley 712: 1824.4/1, 2685.8/1

Harley 741: 2691.3/1

Harley 753: 979/8

Harley 838: 3377/1

Harley 853: 595/16, 3772/12

Harley 874: 1907.5/1

Harley 875: 1459/A6

Harley 913: 718/1, 762/1, 1078/1, 1638/1, 1820/6, 1943/2, 2003/1, 2025/1, 2047/1, 2344/1, 3126/1, 3234/1, 3365/1, 3366/1, 3367/1, 3400/1, 3939/1, 4144/1

Harley 941: 824/19, 1400/3, 3113/3

Harley 957: 2772/1

Harley 978: 3223/1

Harley 984: 704/11

Harley 1002: 430.8/1, 1632.5/1, 3788.5/1, 4028.6/1

Harley 1022: 406/A8, 2017.5/17, 2123/1, 2792/1, 3719/1, 4056/16

Harley 1121: 2320/A10

Harley 1197: 621.5/7, 879.5/7, 1154/1, 1342/19, 2167/20, 3687/7, 4110.5/7, 4150/16

Harley 1205: 3428/42

Harley 1239: 3327/8, 4019/57

Harley 1245: 1168/6, 2219/1

Harley 1251: 302/1, 3580/2

Harley 1260: 620.5/1, 1967.3/1

Harley 1288: 621.5/8, 635.5/1, 853.4/1, 879.5/8, 1186.5/1, 1342/20, 1426.4/1, 2119/18, 2167/21, 3799.6/1, 3860.6/1, 3894.3/1, 4110.5/8, 4150/17

Harley 1304: 2574/18, 4155/4

Harley 1317: 3836.5/1

Harley 1337: 3943/11

Harley 1512: 3816.5/1

Harley 1531: 1683.5/1

Harley 1600: 1293/1, 3422/6

Harley 1620: 2988/10

Harley 1671: 173/3, 3985/5

Harley 1701: 248/3, 778/3, 2780/7

Harley 1703: 2349.5/3, 2831.8/1

Harley 1704: 345/1, 1129/4, 1591/2, 1856/3, 3533/1, 4019/71

Harley 1706: 469/2, 475/1, 505/1, 561/5, 741/2, 880/1, 1126/3, 1416/2, 1460/5, 1721/4, 1746/1, 1748/1, 1781/8, 1815/3, 1854/5, 1937/2, 2352/2, 2585/2, 2770/3, 3040/2, 3143/3, 3262/3, 3685/5, 3793/3, 4160/6

Harley 1717: 4029/6

Harley 1731: 1101/6, 3429/6

Harley 1735: 870.8/1, 970/3, 981.5/1, 1171/1, 1905/6, 3754/5

Harley 1758: 1913/15, 4019/6

Harley 1766: 1168/7

Harley 1770: 3103/6

Harley 1900: 399.5/3, 746.5/3, 1426.6/3, 1637.6/3, 2361.5/3, 2736.2/3, 2831.4/3, 3218.3/3, 4189.5/3

Harley 1944: 716/2

Harley 1948: 716/3

Harley 2013: 716/4

Harley 2124: 716/5

Harley 2150: 716/6

Harley 2202: 1168/12*, 2696/1, 3538.5/1

Harley 2247: 512.5/2, 1173/4

Harley 2250: 82/14, 428/1, 1755/1, 2167/22, 2364/4, 2842/13, 2893/1, 2945/15, 2949/16, 2950/17, 3005/13, 3051/13, 3388/14, 3389/16, 3687/8, 4150/18
Harley 2251: 36/2, 154/2, 168/2, 183/1, 186/4, 199/6, 223/1, 239/9, 357/2, 401/6, 464/3, 500/2, 576/5, 584/1, 614/2, 653/4, 658/7, 698/2, 824/20, 854/16, 860/1, 906/6, 919/3, 935/10, 1037/2, 1056/2, 1152/2, 1168/13*, 1294/6, 1481/3, 1498/2, 1590/1, 1682/1, 1865/5, 1872/2, 1936/1, 1944/4, 2211/3, 2218/3, 2233/15, 2238/1, 2264/3, 2464/7, 2503/1, 2541/3, 2570/2, 2572/2, 2579/2, 2624/5, 2625/7, 2668/1, 2688/2, 2803/1, 2810/1, 2816/2, 2820/2, 2825/2, 3065/4, 3206/1, 3225/2, 3348/6, 3376/1, 3436/1, 3444/5, 3487/2, 3503/4, 3538/3, 3604/2, 3606/2, 3632/22, 3655/3, 3661/8, 3673/3, 3718/2, 3761/2, 3787/5, 3800/2, 3955/10, 4019/72, 4099/4, 4178/3, 4228/1, 4230/5, 4245/5, 4246/8
Harley 2252: 81.5/1, 158.9/1, 301/1, 366.8/1, 432/1, 824/21, 1148/1, 1163/3, 1411/1, 1817/5, 1989/2, 1994/1, 2142/1, 2224/1, 2263.5/1, 2518/1, 2521/1, 2522/1, 2547.3/3, 3087/6, 3088/2, 3172/1, 3609.6/1, 3703.3/1, 3903.5/2, 4040/1, 4175/1, 4253/1
Harley 2253: 105/1, 166/3, 185/1, 205/2, 359/1, 515/1, 694.5/1, 968/1, 1104/1, 1115/2, 1196/1, 1216/1, 1320.5/1, 1365/2, 1394/1, 1395/1, 1407/2, 1449/1, 1461/3, 1504/1, 1678/1, 1705/1, 1747/1, 1861/1, 1889/1, 1894/1, 1921/1, 1922/2, 1974/1, 2039/1, 2066/1, 2078/1, 2166/1, 2207/1, 2236/1, 2287/1, 2359/1, 2604/1, 2649/1, 3155/1, 3211/3, 3236/2, 3310/4, 3874/1, 3939/2, 3963/1, 3989/1, 4037/1, 4177/1, 4194/1
Harley 2255: 178/3, 401/7, 408/1, 447/6, 448/3, 529/4, 915/3, 943/2, 951/4, 953/1, 1019/3, 1037/3, 1050/3, 1130/3, 1168/14*, 1294/7, 1481/4, 1814/2, 1865/6, 1875/2, 2152/1, 2156/3, 2237/1, 2394/4, 2464/8, 2606/2, 2625/8, 2688/3, 2786/1, 2791/9, 2812/4, 2825/3, 3160/1, 3173/1, 3261/1, 3503/5, 3647/1, 3673/4, 3797/1, 3798/5, 3821/1, 3845/10, 4099/5, 4243/4, 4245/6
Harley 2256: 979/9
Harley 2259: 86.5/1, 1181.5/1
Harley 2260: 245/22
Harley 2261: 3632/23
Harley 2274: 2347/3
Harley 2277: 50/9, 56/10, 57/9, 58/9, 59/10, 82/15, 126/8, 184/12, 201/12, 396/2, 409/8, 443/11, 483/12, 578/7, 719/7, 721/12, 791/16, 907/10, 1546/12, 1788/8, 1809/11, 1859/17, 1911/16, 2105/6, 2106/8, 2120/9, 2127/10, 2647/10, 2755/12, 2842/14, 2843/15, 2844/16, 2845/7, 2848/13, 2854/18, 2856/14, 2858/12, 2860/15, 2868/13, 2875/15, 2876/13, 2878/14, 2882/11, 2884/18, 2886/13, 2887/11, 2905/18, 2906/11, 2918/14, 2922/12, 2932/18, 2945/16, 2954/14, 2956/10, 2957/14, 2959/11, 2961/14, 2973/11, 2987/15, 2989/16, 2990/17, 2991/13, 2994/13, 3004/16, 3005/14, 3017/12, 3029/A10, 3033/16, 3041/14, 3042/13, 3046/14, 3048/17, 3050/10, 3051/14, 3055/13, 3059/16, 3060/10, 3063/15, 3064/9, 3266/11, 3388/15, 3389/17, 3664/9, 3766/8, 3767/8
Harley 2278: 530/6, 928/7, 2445/8, 3440/8
Harley 2279: 1934/5
Harley 2280: 3327/9
Harley 2281: 3429/7
Harley 2316: 541/1, 673/1, 994/1, 1133/1, 1139/2, 1251/1, 1391/1, 1684/2, 1799/1, 1818/1, 2056/2, 2069/1, 2125/1, 2145/2, 2150/1, 2158/1, 2319/1, 2818/1, 3079/1, 3108/1, 3621/1, 3717/1, 3770.5/1, 3901/1, 3902/1, 4079/1
Harley 2320: 1171/2, 3580/5
Harley 2321: 34.8/4, 63.8/1, 397/1, 1174.5/1, 1400/4, 1867.5/1, 2785.5/1, 2818.3/1, 3318.8/3, 4049.5/1, 4079.6/4
Harley 2330: 352/3
Harley 2338: 646/2, 3945/1
Harley 2339: 255/1, 620/2, 1126/4, 1758/1, 1781/9, 1815/4, 1983/1, 2714/6, 2770/4, 3040/3, 3262/4, 3555/1, 3685/6, 4200/4
Harley 2341: 3571/1
Harley 2346: 1718/6
Harley 2376: 1459/C11
Harley 2377: 3429/8
Harley 2379: 3687/9, 4150/19
Harley 2380: 3309/1, 3597/1, 3612/3, 3714/1

(continued overleaf)

London, British Lib.

Harley 2382: 173/4, 1157/1, 2119/38, 2165/4, 2464/9, 2574/19, 2613.5/1, 4019/73, 4019/84, 4110.5/9, 4154/6
Harley 2383: 621.5/9, 879.5/9, 2063/1, 2079/1
Harley 2386: 821/3
Harley 2388: 750/2, 1136.3/1, 1342/21
Harley 2389: 4126.5/1
Harley 2391: 25/7, 26/7, 32/7, 45/6, 46/5, 47/7, 79/5, 89/5, 284/6, 286/6, 288/4, 289/8, 291/5, 306/6, 314/7, 348/3, 416/4, 485/5, 1129/5, 1144/3, 1464/6, 1469/3, 1482/7, 1641/5, 1642/6, 1643/6, 1645/5, 1646/5, 1647/5, 1817/6, 1856/4, 2094/5, 2124/2, 2859/3, 3015/2, 3288/5, 3289/6, 3296/1, 3298/5, 3317/6, 3547/2, 3784/4, 3816/7, 3865/6, 3954/6
Harley 2392: 3327/10
Harley 2394: 3428/43
Harley 2398: 2320/C6, 3397/9
Harley 2399: 250/1, 711.5/1, 1985/2, 3294/1, 4232/1
Harley 2403: 462/7, 4068.3/6
Harley 2406: 241/4, 493.5/1, 1771/1, **not 1790.5/1, *see* Cambridge Univ. Lib. Dd.8.2.**
Harley 2407: 1203/2, 1205/1, 1364/1, 1438/1, 1558/1, 2330/1, 2656/21, 2784/8, 3253/3, 3528/2
Harley 2409: 1188/4
Harley 2417: 462/8, 4068.3/7
Harley 2445: 1703/7
Harley 2851: 1703/8
Harley 2869: 1147/1, 1632/1
Harley 2888: 1276.8/1
Harley 2942: 2348/1, 3220/1
Harley 3038: 685/1, 4179/1
Harley 3352: 3922/3*
Harley 3362: 16/2, 19/2, 430.5/2, 808/2, 906/7, 1251.5/3, 1396/1, 2249/1, 3122/6, 3199.5/2, 3292.3/2, 3318.8/4, 3322.5/1, 3502.5/2, 3769.5/1, 3792.5/4, 3894.6/3, 4079.3/3, 4079.8/2
Harley 3383: 1605/3
Harley 3486: 1168/8
Harley 3490: 2662/A15
Harley 3528: 2668/2
Harley 3542: 1214/3, 1214/4, 3423/1
Harley 3724: 2703/2, 3104/1
Harley 3725: 1608/1, 3341/1
Harley 3730: 710/13
Harley 3760: 807.5/1, 853.8/1, 1175/1
Harley 3775: 4184/19
Harley 3776: 3237/1
Harley 3810: 622/4, 843/1, 1502/11, 1961/4, 3087/7, 3184/2, 3198/1, 3785/1, 3868/2, 4275/1
Harley 3835: 1427/1
Harley 3862: 2574/20
Harley 3865: 3703/1
Harley 3869: 2168/1, 2200/2, 2662/C6
Harley 3909: 1755/2
Harley 3943: 3327/11
Harley 3952: 1505/1, 2574/21
Harley 3954: 250/2, 404/3, 1459/B13, 1523/1, 1901/2, 1986/2, 1988/1, 2045/2, 2059/2, 2062/2
Harley 4011: 199/7, 824/22, 1168/15*, 1514/1, 1721/5, 1728/3, 2192/1, 2233/16, 2574/22, 3491/5, 3655/5
Harley 4012: 497/1, 1779/1, 3038/1, 3207/2, 3827/2
Harley 4196: 25/8, 26/8, 32/8, 41/1, 46/6, 47/8, 53/2, 75/2, 97/6, 128/2, 170/3, 198/2, 287/2, 288/5, 289/9, 314/8, 316/2, 319/2, 330/2, 332/2, 386/2, 388/2, 389/2, 390/2, 391/2, 392/2, 393/2, 394/2, 512/2, 539/4, 599/2, 626/2, 627/2, 677/2, 713/2, 807/2, 876/2, 948/2, 1006/1, 1208/1, 1209/1, 1482/8, 1494/5, 1516/2, 1517/1, 1519/6, 1520/2, 1547/2, 1572/2, 1584/2, 1612/2, 1616/2, 1623/2, 1641/12, 1643/7, 1645/6, 1660/2, 1668/2, 1670/2, 1671/2, 1689/2, 1698/2, 1716/2, 1773/2, 1792/2, 1800/2, 2022/2, 2084/4, 2144/2, 2199/1, 2637/1, 2638/2, 2639/1, 2715/1, 2722/2, 2723/2, 2840/1, 2846/1, 2847/2, 2857/2, 2869/2, 2917/2, 2920/2, 2923/1, 2925/2, 2931/2, 2936/6, 2938/5, 2939/5, 2943/2, 2946/2, 2947/2, 2948/2, 2962/1, 2964/2, 2966/2, 2970/5, 2971/6, 2975/2, 2979/2, 2980/2, 2981/2, 2982/2, 2983/2, 2984/2, 2985/2, 2986/2, 2996/5, 2997/2, 2998/2, 3000/2, 3004.5/2, 3006/2, 3010/2, 3014/2, 3016/2, 3018/6, 3022/2, 3023/2, 3024/2, 3025/2, 3032/2, 3043/1, 3044/2, 3045/2, 3047/2, 3054/2, 3056/1, 3062/2, 3166/2, 3167/2, 3176/2, 3177/2, 3178/2, 3290/5, 3392/2, 3394/2, 3425/2, 3428/44, 3516/2, 3519/2, 3548/2, 3592/7, 3602/1, 3617/2, 3758/2, 3830/2, 3840/2, 3865/7, 3933/6, 3934/2, 3935/2, 3941/2, 3953/2,

3974/2, 3977/2, 3978/2, 3979/2,
3981/2, 3982/2, 3984/2, 4002/2,
4032/2, 4048/2, 4049/2, 4250/4
Harley 4197: 1168/9
Harley 4203: 1168/10
Harley 4205: 444/9
Harley 4260: 2574/23
Harley 4294: 772/1, 2072.4/1,
3119.5/1, 3776/4, 3782/1, 4216/1
Harley 4486: 2000.5/2, 3985/6
Harley 4690: 1979/4, 3539/1
Harley 4733: 854/17, 1881/6,
3501/2, 3955/11
Harley 4789: 33/4
Harley 4800: 1297/10
Harley 4826: 928/8, 935/11,
1875/3, 2229/25, 2445/9, 2806.5/1,
3440/9
Harley 4866: 2229/26
Harley 4912: 3327/12
Harley 5036: 1417.5/1, 3226/3
Harley 5086: 1576/1, 3318/2,
3793/4
Harley 5259: 2238.5/1, 3322.3/1
Harley 5272: 2447/3, 2574/24
Harley 5312: 4129/8
Harley 5369: 3568.5/1
Harley 5396: 463/2, 884/1,
987.5/1, 1226/2, 1319/1, 1338/1,
1718/7, 1877/2, 1897/2, 1899/3,
1982/2, 2052/6, 2119/39, 2615/2,
3685/7, 3845/11, 3883/3, 3932/1
Harley 5398: 995.3/1
Harley 5401: 824/23, 1275/1
Harley 5908: 4019/77
Harley 5927: 306.5/2
Harley 5977: 245/38
Harley 6041: 1459/A7
Harley 6149: 800/2
Harley 6223: 1162/2
Harley 6580: 1342/22, 1491/13,
2119/19, 2167/23, 4150/20
Harley 6641: 3782.5/2
Harley 6718: 827.8/1
Harley 6848: 4184/8
Harley 6909: 399/9a
Harley 6919: 3584/2
Harley 6923: 3428/45
Harley 7184: 2662/C7
Harley 7322: 33.8/1, 101/1, 102/1,
155/1, 187/1, 221/1, 502/1, 592/1,
798/10, 819/1, 827.5/3, 850/1,
995.8/1, 1131/1, 1137/1, 1217/1,
1267/1, 1269/1, 1466/1, 1585/1,
1615/1, 1634/1, 1639/1, 1822/12,
1847/1, 1958/1, 2008/1, 2014/1,
2074/2, 2133/1, 2141/1, 2155/1,
2167/24, 2382/1, 2646/1, 2695/1,
3106/1, 3219/1, 3278/1, 3311/1,

3325/1, 3353/1, 3357/1, 3411/1,
3506/1, 3511/1, 3610/1, 3644/1,
3646/1, 3647.5/1, 3680/1, 3734/1,
3858/1, 3867/1, 3907/1, 4033/1,
4045/1, 4107/1, 4203/1, 4208/1,
4224/1, 4259/1, 4273/1
Harley 7332: 52/2, 734.8/5
Harley 7333: 370/3, 809/11,
854/18, 860/2, 875/3, 913/6,
1388/3, 2081/5, 2128/2, 2229/27,
2238.5/2, 2290/1, 2662/D6, 2749/1,
2804/1, 3190/7, 3322.3/2, 3348/7,
3412/13, 3437/3, 3440/10, 3504/2,
3632/24, 3670/6, 3711/1, 3787/6,
3808/1, 3955/12, 4019/34, 4074/1
Harley 7334: 1913/16, 4019/7
Harley 7335: 4019/35
Harley 7358: 2024/1, 4219/1
Harley 7371: 3449/2
Harley 7578: 231/1, 239/10, 551/1,
674/5, 1269.5/1, 1635/1, 2029/3,
2218/4, 2626/1, 2756/7, 3097.6/1,
3190/8, 3348/8, 3437/4, 3487/3,
3504/3, 3559.8/1, 3656/4, 3687/16,
3749/1, 3914/2, 4230/6
Harley Charters 58.C.14: 1727/10
Lansdowne 96: 985.5/1, 1513.5/1
Lansdowne 197: 399/2, 1377/2
Lansdowne 204: 710/8
Lansdowne 205: 4071/1
Lansdowne 207: 3857.5/1
Lansdowne 210: 1811/1, 3632/25,
3642.5/1
Lansdowne 239: 1844.5/4
Lansdowne 269: 3300/5
Lansdowne 285: 935/12, 1224/1,
1929/3
Lansdowne 344: 1342/23, 1491/14,
2119/20, 2167/25, 3373/3, 4150/21
Lansdowne 348: 3429/9
Lansdowne 379: 78/1, 4065/2
Lansdowne 388: 262/1, 1132.5/1
Lansdowne 398: 1459/B3B
Lansdowne 409: 199/8
Lansdowne 418: 3126/2, 4280/1
**(transcript from missing part of
Harley 913)**
Lansdowne 455: 2017.5/18,
4056/17
Lansdowne 470: 4148/7
Lansdowne 680: 3422/7, 3848/13
Lansdowne 699: 36/3, 77/3,
512.5/3, 658/8, 809/12, 824/24,
875/4, 1168/16*, 1481/5, 1875/4,
2233/17, 2590/4, 2606/3, 2784/9,
2825/4, 3632/26, 3661/9, 3748/2,
4112/4
Lansdowne 762: 285.5/1, 324/3,
363/1, 365/4, 734.8/6, 761/1,

(continued overleaf)

765/1, 864.5/1, 892.5/1, 1015/1, 1214.9/3, 1392/1, 1488/3, 1570.5/1, 1655.5/1, 1933.5/3, 2633/1, 2668/3, 2793.5/1, 3308.5/4, 3375/1, 3412.3/1, 3510/1, 3513.5/1, 3521.5/1, 3632/27, 3780/1, 3818/2, 3903.5/3, 3945/2, 4018/4, 4029/7, 4101/1, 4103/1, 4106/2, 4117/3, 4148/8
Lansdowne 793: 772/2
Lansdowne 796: 921/1
Lansdowne 851: 1913/17, 4019/8
Lansdowne 1176: 4113/11
Loan 29/333 (Portland): 270/1, 317.5/1
Royal 2 A.XVII: 1502/6
Royal 2 B.X: 1750/1, 1770/1
Royal 2 D.XXXVII: 3083/2
Royal 2 F.VIII: 2687/4, 3963/2
Royal 4 A.XIV: 3896/1
Royal 5 A.V: 2233/18
Royal 5 A.VI: 2167/26, 2320/B11, 3648/2
Royal 5 F.VII: 598/3, 2988/11, 3031/1
Royal 6 B.IX: 2824/1
Royal 7 A.VI: 1871/1
Royal 7 A.VIII: 4061/1
Royal 7 A.IX: 4008/C14
Royal 7 C.I: 3901/2
Royal 7 C.IX: 3249.6/1
Royal 7 E.IV: 2700.5/1, 4202/3
Royal 8 A.IV: 4181/7
Royal 8 A.XXI: 2064/1, 2229/28
Royal 8 C.I: 621.5/10, 879.5/10, 4110.5/10
Royal 8 C.VII: 858.8/1
Royal 8 C.XII: 173/5, 756/1, 1307/2, 1400/5, 4035/13
Royal 8 D.X: 2039.8/1, 3647.3/1
Royal 8 D.XIII (18 D.XIII in *IMEV*): 3512/1
Royal 8 E.V: 750/3, 1342/24, 2119/21, 2167/27, 3687/10
Royal 8 E.XVII: 2817/1, 4202/4
Royal 8 F.II: 3211/4
Royal 8 F.III: 4217/1
Royal 8 F.VI: 2099/1, 3373/2
Royal 8 F.VII: 78.5/1, 1129/6, 1479/1, 2692/1, 3116/1
Royal 8 F.XII: 1502/12
Royal 9 C.II: 1254/1, 1421/1, 4013/1
Royal 11 C.III: 4094/1
Royal 12 B.XXV: 624/4, 3771/2
Royal 12 C.XII: 1105/A1, 2320/A11, 2787/4
Royal 12 C.XIV: 2172/1
Royal 12 E.I: 2079.5/1, 3211/5, 3964/1
Royal 12 E.XVI: 81.5/2, 106.5/2, 430.5/3, 1989/3, 3341/2, 3767.5/1
Royal 12 F.XIII: 1169/1
Royal 13 D.I: 3653/1
Royal 13 E.IX: 1796/1
Royal 14 C.VII (*IMEV* says no MS extant): 1252/1, 1335/1, 2830/1, 4284.8/1
Royal 16 F.II: 922/1, 2246/1, 2289/1
Royal 17 A.I: 4149/1
Royal 17 A.III: 1293/2
Royal 17 A.VIII: 624/5
Royal 17 A.XVI: 705/2, 1033/1, 1063/1, 1467/1, 1626/1, 1640/1, 3943/12
Royal 17 A.XXVII: 908/1, 1030/3, 1370/3, 2119/40, 2577/6, 3305.8/1, 3570.5/2, 4098/1
Royal 17 A.XXXII: 992/1, 1162.6/1, 1256.5/1, 1586/1
Royal 17 B.XVII: 190/2, 230/1, 244/5, 906/8, 1014/1, 1101/7, 1178/1, 2017.5/19, 2319/2, 2787/5, 3238/3, 3274/1, 3507/5, 4006/1
Royal 17 B.XLIII: 973/1, 1724/3, 2086/1
Royal 17 B.XLVII: 113/1, 824/25, 854/19, 2490/1, 3609.6/2, 3893/2, 4148/9
Royal 17 C.VIII: 245/23
Royal 17 C.XIV: 2229/29
Royal 17 C.XVII: 859/1, 961/7, 1052/1, 1174/1, 1189/1, 1693/1, 1961/5, 1976/1, 2990/18, 2994/14, 3153/1, 3268/2, 3428/a, 3850/1
Royal 17 D.VI: 513/4, 932/1, 1088.5/2, 1151/10, 1561/6, 2229/30, 2257/1, 3121/5, 3909/2, 4072/6
Royal 17 D.XV: 1514/2, 1913/18, 2808/1, 4019/36
Royal 17 D.XVIII: 1151/8, 2195.3/1, 2229/31, 3831/2
Royal 17 D.XIX: 2229/32
Royal 17 D.XX: 399/3, 1377/3, 3577/1
Royal 18 A.V: 3429/10
Royal 18 A.VI: 1170/1
Royal 18 A.X: 351/4, 561/6, 964/1, 2481/1, 2864/1, 3415/1
Royal 18 A.XIII: 1597/15, 1865/7
Royal 18 A.XVII: 663/2, 1165/2, 663/2, 1459/C12, 3397/10
Royal 18 B.XXII: 81.5/3, 1165/3, 1390.3/1
Royal 18 B.XXIII: 548.3/1, 664.5/1, 837/1, 853.6/1, 1277/1, 1281.5/1, 1509.5/1, 1955/1, 3397/11, 3645.5/1, 3729.5/1, 4201/1, 4202/5

(continued overleaf)

London, British Lib.

Sloane 2352: 1150.3/3
Sloane 2452: 1168/17*
Sloane 2457: 305.5/1, 1952.5/1, 2623.8/1, 2627/10, 3848/19, 4154.8/1
Sloane 2464: 935/14
Sloane 2478: 180/1
Sloane 2532: 3772/17
Sloane 2577: 1168/18*
Sloane 2578: 365/5, 734.8/7, 4006/3, 4008/Ab, 4008/Ac, 4029/9
Sloane 2584: 624/7, 1605/1, 3422/10, 3634.5/1
Sloane 2593: 20/2, 72/1, 80/1, 117/1, 118/1, 354/4, 356/1, 361/2, 377/1, 378/1, 454/1, 527/1, 562/5, 725/1, 739/1, 1020/1, 1230/2, 1268/1, 1299/1, 1302/1, 1303/1, 1317/1, 1351/1, 1367/1, 1417/1, 1433/1, 1522/1, 1568/1, 1574/1, 1575/3, 1627/1, 1650/2, 1662/1, 1739/1, 1785/1, 1892/3, 1893/1, 1896/1, 1938/1, 2061/1, 2103/1, 2111/1, 2113/1, 2339/3, 2384/1, 2675/1, 2730/1, 2747/1, 2771/2, 3034/1, 3058/1, 3070/3, 3085/1, 3329/2, 3343/2, 3347/1, 3472/1, 3537/1, 3566/1, 3643/1, 3658/1, 3700.5/1, 3707/2, 3733/1, 3864/1, 3877/2, 3920/1, 3959/1, 4219/2, 4279/1, 4281/1
Sloane 3153: 1293/4, 3422/20
Sloane 3160: 231.5/1, 1603/2, 1680/1, 3771/3, 3848/20, 3958.5/1, 4181/8
Sloane 3215: 77/5, 3754/6
Sloane 3285: 4182/3
Sloane 3292: 4184/10
Sloane 3501: 1176.8/1, 1333 **(first line as title)**, 2261.6/1
Sloane 3534: 824/29, 4181/9
Sloane 3548: 48/1
Sloane 3580B: 2666/7, 3249/23, 3257/8, 3772/18
Sloane 3667: 410/5, 1276/12, 2666/8, 2826/5, 3249/24, 3257/9
Sloane 3688: 3249/25, 3721/11
Sloane 3747: 410/4, 545/1, 2656/22, 2666/2, 3249/26, 3257/10, 3257/2, 3618/1, 4017/8
Sloane 4031: 1168/14, 4029/10, 4257/1
Stowe 39: 91.8/2, 672/2, 1387/2, 1834/1 1637.6/4, 2361.5/4, 2736.2/4, 2831.4/4, 3218.3/4, 4189.5/4
Stowe 65: 399.5/4, 746.5/4,
Stowe 69: 3632/29
Stowe 95: 1426.6/4
Stowe 393: 1543/1
Stowe 620: 4184/20
Stowe 850: 324/7
Stowe 949: 184/13, 201/13, 213/B4, 721/13, 1801/4, 2743/1, 2848/14, 2870/10, 2873/11, 2875/16, 2882/12, 2886/14, 2887/12, 2891/4, 2894/11, 2897/8, 2899/10, 2900/6, 2922/13, 2932/19, 2954/15, 2958/10, 2961/15, 2973/12, 3005/15, 3029/A11, 3033/17, 3049/4, 3050/11, 3055/14, 3059/17, 3063/16, 3064/10, 3192/1, 3354/1, 3452/7, 3559/3, 3973/8, 3997/3, 4171/4, 4173/3
Stowe 950: 2662/A17
Stowe 951: 245/25, 4105/1
Stowe 952: 2395/1, 4265/3
Stowe 953: 3193/1
Stowe 982: 824/26, 2233/19
Stowe 1055: 4184/21
Yates Thompson 13 (olim Yates Thompson 57): 1270/2
Yates Thompson 47 (first two entries have no number in *IMEV*): 928/9, 2445/11, 3440/12
unidentified, not Harley 2756: 2778/1

London, College of Arms
Arundel 8: 907/12, 3029/A1
Arundel 14: 310/A6, 313/A6, 814/7, 841/7, 2686/A6, 2754/A7, 3352/7, 3799.3/2, 4113/15
Arundel 22: 3139/3
Arundel 27: 60/1, 371/1
Arundel 41: 2686/A7
Arundel 57: 2153/7, 3428/56, 3976/6
Arundel 58: 444/11, 727/C16, 1979/6, 3539/2, 3632/32
Arundel 61: 310/A7, 313/A7, 814/8, 841/8, 2754/A8, 3352/8
Arundel 65: 2662/A20
I.7: 3118.5/1
Schedule 3 no.16 (formerly box 21 no.16): 3910/1

London, Corporation of London Records Office, formerly Guildhall
3133: 1929/4, 3799/4
Great Chronicle: 1933.5/4
Liber Horn: 2698/11, 4113/16
Liber de antiquis legibus: 322/1

London, Dr Williams's Lib.
Anc.3: 621.5/12, 879.5/12, 4110.5/12

London, Dulwich College
22: 3194/3
24: 778/4

London, Gray's Inn
 12: 635.5/3, 853.4/3, 1147.8/2,
 1426.4/3, 1850/1, 2689.5/1,
 3218.5/2, 3799.6/3, 3860.6/3,
 3894.3/3
 15: 3254/11
 20: 1184/8, 2845/8

**London, Guildhall, now Corporation of
London Records Office**

London, Inner Temple
 Petyt 511.7: 310/B10, 313/B10,
 718.5/1, 814/11, 841/11, 1995/3,
 2686/B10, 2754/B11, 3291.5/1,
 3352/11
 Petyt 511.11: 3748/3
 Petyt 524: 2516/17

London, Lambeth Palace
 3: 1661/1
 6: 4056.8/1
 51: 2988/12
 78: 174/1, 1935/14, 2167/32,
 3239/1, 3408/13
 84: 2657/1
 117 (no number in *IMEV*): 1842.5/4
 120: 861/1
 131: 310/B11, 313/B11, 814/12,
 841/12, 1995/4, 2686/B11,
 2754/B12, 3291.5/2, 3352/12
 180: 2773/1
 223: 82/17, 184/14, 213/B6,
 791/18, 1092/1, 1801/5, 1859/19,
 1911/18, 2680/1, 2743/2, 2837/4,
 2839/17, 2842/16, 2848/15,
 2850/18, 2856/16, 2858/14,
 2861/3, 2866/18, 2868/15, 2870/11,
 2871/3, 2873/12, 2874/13, 2875/17,
 2878/16, 2880/19, 2882/13,
 2884/20, 2886/15, 2887/13,
 2889/16, 2893/2, 2894/13, 2896/5,
 2897/9, 2899/11, 2904/1, 2910/18,
 2912/15, 2915/9, 2918/16, 2921/2,
 2922/14, 2932/21, 2949/18,
 2950/19, 2951/16, 2954/16, 2955/2,
 2957/16, 2958/11, 2959/12,
 2961/16, 2973/13, 2987/17,
 2990/20, 3004/18, 3005/16,
 3017/14, 3026/17, 3029/A14,
 3033/18, 3035/17, 3039/2, 3041/16,
 3046/15, 3048/19, 3050/12,
 3051/16, 3053/5, 3055/15, 3059/18,
 3063/17, 3064/16, 3067/18,
 3068/19, 3159/3, 3290.5/1, 3335/2,
 3354/2, 3384/12, 3388/17,
 3389/19, 3452/9, 3559/4, 3813/16,
 3973/9, 3985/9, 3997/5, 4171/3,
 4173/4, 4266/17
 256: 1168/18
 259: 686/1, 1165/4, 4187/1

 260: 25/11, 26/12, 32/9, 43/5,
 45/9, 46/8, 47/9, 79/7, 89/7, 97/9,
 132/6, 284/9, 286/9, 288/7,
 289/11, 290/5, 291/8, 306/9,
 314/10, 323/8, 348/4, 485/8,
 777/6, 1117/6, 1118/7, 1136/7,
 1144/6, 1464/9, 1469/6, 1482/11,
 1494/8, 1518/4, 1519/8, 1521/7,
 1641/7, 1642/9, 1643/10, 1645/7,
 1646/8, 1647/8, 1648/7, 1657/7,
 1862/6, 1912/6, 2084/6, 2094/7,
 2248/1, 2301/7, 2859/5, 2907/5,
 2926/5, 2927/5, 2930/7, 2934/2,
 2935/5, 2936/7, 2937/8, 2938/6,
 2939/7, 2940/5, 2941/4, 2967/5,
 2968/5, 2970/7, 2971/8, 2976/7,
 2978/6, 2996/9, 2999/5, 3002/7,
 3003/8, 3008/4, 3009/7, 3012/7,
 3013/6, 3018/10, 3020/6, 3021/7,
 3288/7, 3289/8, 3290/8, 3296/2,
 3298/6, 3317/9, 3393/5, 3395/7,
 3428/57, 3492/7, 3547/4, 3588/3,
 3590/6, 3591/7, 3592/9, 3683/7,
 3708/7, 3738/7, 3739/7, 3740/7,
 3741/5, 3784/6, 3790/7, 3791/7,
 3816/10, 3829/6, 3857/4, 3865/9,
 3933/7, 3954/9, 4226/8
 265: 3581/1, 4273.8/1
 306: 252/1, 658/10, 700/1, 868/1,
 897/2, 941/3, 1172/4, 1555/2,
 1653/3, 1690/4, 1789/1, 2052/7,
 2247/1, 2397/1, 2714/10, 2789/3,
 3127/1, 3171/3, 3291/1, 3612/6,
 3632/35, 3880/1, 4148/11
 331: 979/11
 344: 222/2, 653/6, 809/16, 1830/1,
 2483/2, 2574/34, 2791/10, 3190/11,
 4246/10
 390: 1863/1
 408: 406/B1
 432: 2599/1
 444: 824/37
 487: 1272/6, 2709/1
 491: 851.6/1, 1566/2, 1583/6,
 1815/5, 3040/4, 3262/5, 3428/58,
 4064/2
 492: 3428/59
 522: 2320/A13
 523: 3157/1
 541: 874/1, 1666/1, 1719.5/1,
 1736/1, 1947/1, 3454/1
 545: 1502/7
 546: 1435/1
 557: 207/1, 3825/2
 559: 248/5, 984/1, 1030/4, 1325/1,
 1372/5, 1684/4, 1708/3, 1727/11,
 1761/7, 2112/1, 2116/2, 2118/3,
 2119/44, 2451/1, 2512/1, 3231/7,
 3883/5

(continued overleaf)

London, Lambeth Palace

560: 172/5, 4089/1
742: 3928/19
783 (738 in *IMEV*): 2305/1a
853: 349/2, 404/4, 547/1, 560/2, 671/3, 744/2, 880/2, 1028/1, 1032/3, 1259/7, 1379/5, 1418/2, 1454/3, 1460/7, 1463/2, 1511/3, 1570/1, 1727/12, 1769/1, 1781/13, 1891/2, 2007/B1, 2040/2, 2233/21, 2714/11, 3087/10, 3195/1, 3225/3, 3533/4, 3612/7, 3985/10, 3992/3, 4155/5, 4160/8
878: 1721/6
935: 242/1
Carew 617: 573/1
Carew 623 (Book of Howth): 632/1, 674/9 **(item not found)**

London, Lincoln's Inn
Hale 74: 3772/21
Hale 135: 360/1
Hale 150: 683/3, 1162/4, 1459/A8, 1690/5, 3139/4
Hale 186 (no number in *IMEV*): 2691.3/3
Misc.2 (Misc.46) (so *MMBL*, *IMEV* says class V, 46): 4148/12

London, Public Record Office
C 47/34/1/4: 4215/4
C 47/34/1/5: 2304/15, 2872/16, 2912/16, 2950/21, 3813/17, 4266/18
C 47/34/1/12: 463/3, 1892/4, 2774/2
C 47/37/11: 2182.3/1, 2236.5/1, 2437.5/1, 2657.5/1
C 47/37/12: 3768.2/1
C 47/39/15: 1936.5/1
DL 41/6/1 (*IMEV* DL A.23): 4183/3
E 163/22/1 (*SUP* 163/22/1/1): 2293.5/1
E 163/22/2: 3706.9/1
Exchequer Roll, K.R. Proc. bundle 1, unlocated: 3940/2
KB 9/144, m.31: 1543/2
SC 2/175/41: 1531.5/1
SP 1/246: 1414.5/1, 1620.5/1
State Papers Henry VIII, unlocated: 4008/A8, 4056.5/1
Treasury Receipt of Exchequer B 2 8, unlocated: 3456.5/1

London, Royal College of Physicians
388 (13): 4019/44

London, Sion College
Arc.L.40.2/E.23, now Tokyo, Takamiya 22
Arc.L.40.2/E.25: 512/4, 557.3/1, 771/3, 3428/64
Arc.L.40.2/E.44: 239/13

London, Society of Antiquaries
101: 824/38, 2627/13, 3491/6, 3756/1
134: 1597/19, 2229/38, 2574/35, 2662/A22, 2742/10 687 **(no number in *IMEV*)**: 621.5/14
687: 879.5/14, 1459/A14, 3428/69, 4110.5/14

London, St Paul's Cathedral Lib.
9.D.xix (=8 in *MMBL*): 1358/1, 2765/1, 3770/1, 4036/1

London, Univ. of London
278: 727/B12
278: 2794.8/1
657 (olim Helmingham Hall LJ I.7): 29/2, 1286/9, 1342/33, 1491/21, 1980/1, 2067/1, 2068/1, 2167/39
S.L.,V 17 (no number in *IMEV*): 1459/C16, 3194/4
S.L.,V 88: 1459/C17

London, University College
Fragment Ang.1: 2662/D9

London, Victoria & Albert Museum
Dyce 33: 2464/15
Dyce 45: 554.5/1, 607.3/1, 1018.5/1, 1455.5/1, 1494.5/1, 3079.7/2, 3228.3/1, 3530.5/1, 3598.5/1, 4162.5/1
Reid 7: 1752/3, 3477.6/1
Reid (no number in *IMEV*, not found): 3580/7

London, Wellcome Historical Medical Lib.
41: 113.8/1, 4181/17
225: 1322.5/1
404: 624/10
405: 2323.5/1
406: 624/11, 824/50, 3754/7, 3848/25
411: 824/51, 1905/7
519: 2656/26, 3249/29, 3721/12
542: 624/12, 1293/7, 3422/11
580: 3772/23
632: 1703/12, 3443/6
673: 576/7, 705/3 **(1493 in *IMEV*)**, 3173.5/1, 3721.8/1, 3985/13
692: 1364.5/5
693: 1364.5/6

London, Westminster Abbey
20: 30/2
27: 906/14, 4008/A9, 4029/16
34.3 (Cathedral in *IMEV*): 1355.5/1

London, Westminster School
3: 197.8/7 **(no number in *IMEV*)**, 754.5/1, 1367.5/8 **(no number in *IMEV*)**, 2017.5/24, 2250/8, 2270/8, 4056/23

Longleat, Marquess of Bath
15: 2574/36
29: 197.8/9, 200/2, 229/3, 241/5, 1367.5/9, 1761/9, 2007/2, 2017.5/27, 2119/46, 2121/1, 2169/1, 2250/9, 2270/10, 3191/1, 3238/7, 3502/5, 3730/3, 3743/1, 4035/16, 4056/26
30: 896/1, 914/8, 1045/2, 1370/5, 1721/7, 1727/14, 1748/2, 1761/10, 1831/1, 1961/10, 2118/4, 2119/47, 2306/1, 2352/3, 2469/3, 2473/1, 2577/13, 2711/2, 3305.8/3, 4200/7
31: 3428/79
32: 2320/C10
53 (no number in *IMEV*): 3799/5
55: 1113/1, 3205/1
174 (no number in *IMEV*): 1910/1
176 ? (no number in *IMEV*, not found): 970/7
178 (no number in *IMEV*): 595/22, 3772/24
252A (no number in *IMEV*): 1842.5/5
253: 2766/2, 3553.8/1
254: 665/1, 1168/22
256: 923/2, 2812/5, 3947/2
257: 944/2, 3928/23, 4019/65, 4019/78
258: 232/2, 851/9, 913/7, 1086/6, 1528/3, 1548/1, 2756/9, 2784/13, 3412/15, 3670/8

Lyme Hall, (Legh)
deposited in Rylands Lib.: 1011.5/2

Madrid, Escorial
Castellanos G.II.19: 2662/A33
iv.a.24: 2782/1

Maggs Cat.580 item 449, now Princeton, Taylor Medieval 13

Maidstone, Museum
6: 1781/18
A.13: 433/4, 695/3, 2070/5, 3246/1

Manchester, Central Lib.
822.11 C2 (no number in *IMEV*): 716/10

Manchester, Chetham Lib.
6690: 1732/2, 1780/2, 2017.5/21, 4056/20
6696: 2662/A19
6709: 439/6, 527.5/1, 927.5/1, 2445/10, 2459/1, 2574/31, 2592/4, 3440/11, 3673/6, 3830.5/1, 4019/74, 4019/85
8008: 3428/55
8009: 854/24, 983/1, 1514/5, 1751/1, 1993/B1, 2119/43, 2165/6, 2392/2, 2619/3, 2635/1, 3955/14
11379: 399.5/7, 1637.6/7, 2361.5/7, 2736.2/7, 2831.4/7, 3218.3/7

Manchester, John Rylands Lib.
Crawford 1: 2742/9
Eng.1: 2516/18
Eng.2: 524/2, 1168/19
Eng.50: 1101/10, 1193/3, 3428/62
Eng.51: 3428/61, 3755/5
Eng.90: 3428/60 = also 3428/68
(olim Ashburnham App.243)
Eng.113: 2227/1, 4019/11, 4062/1
Eng.955: 3491/15
Lat.165: 854.5/1, 1808.5/1
Lat.176: 4184/15
Lat.201: 2742/15, 2820/7, 3687/12, 3943/15, 3985/11
Lat.228: 1946.5/1, 4014.8/1, 4064.5/1
Lat.341: 1342/29, 2167/33
Lat.394: 37.5/5, 95.5/1, 190.3/2, 228.5/2, 475.8/3, 548.8/1, 672.3/2, 735.3/2, 769.5/1, 817.5/1, 906/20, 908.2/2, 1137.5/2, 1147.2/2, 1149.5/3, 1173/6, 1223.5/2, 1251.5/4, 1635.5/1, 1998.5/2, 2668.5/3, 2691.5/2, 3167.6/2, 3199.5/3, 3207.5/2, 3209/4, 3292.3/3, 3318.8/5, 3372.4/1, 3464.5/3, 3522.5/2, 3706.2/3, 3792.5/5, 3815.5/3, 3860.3/2, 3927.3/2, 4020.6/2, 4034.6/5, 4079.3/4, 4079.6/5, 4128.2/2, 4128.6/2, 4145.5/2, 4176.5/3, 4180.6/2, 4202/6
Lat.395: 339/1, 1460/8, 4163/1, 4189/2
Lyme Hall deposit (Legh), Scottish Feilde: 1011.5/2

Marlborough Vicarage
William of Nassington, Speculum vite: 245/31

Massachusetts Hist.Soc.
Winthrop 20 c: 1150.3/4, 1276/13, 2308.3/1, 2420.5/1, 2656/24, 3249/32, 3772/26, 4017/10

Melbourne, State Lib. of Victoria
***096/G94**: 34.5/1, 233/11, 239/16, 263/11, 528.5/1, 540/9, 1041.3/1, 1242/11, 1243/10, 1244/11, 1245/10, 1246/11, 1247/11, 1248/10, 1249.5/1, 1249/11, 1296/10, 1490.5/1, 1719/10, 2271.4/1, 2384.5/1, 2428/11, 2440.5/1, 2533.5/1

Merton 28, Breslauer Cat.90 item 24, now Chicago, Newberry f.33.7

Meyerstein, Sotheby 17 Dec 1952

Meyerstein, Sotheby 17 Dec 1952, lot 466, now Princeton, Taylor Medieval 3

Minneapolis, Minnesota Univ. Lib.
Z.822.N.81: 25/14, 32/12, 40/9, 43/8, 45/12, 46/11, 47/12, 79/10, 89/10, 97/12, 208/1, 284/12, 286/12, 288/10, 289/15, 290/8, 291/11, 306/12, 314/13, 385/6, 416/8, 1117/9, 1118/11, 1136/10, 1144/8, 1469/8, 1482/14, 1494/11, 1518/7, 1519/11, 1521/10, 1641/11, 1643/13, 1645/10, 1646/11, 1648/10, 1657/10, 1862/9, 1912/9, 2084/9, 2094/10, 2301/10, 2858/15, 2859/8, 2904/2, 2926/8, 2927/8, 2930/10, 2934/3, 2935/8, 2936/10, 2937/11, 2938/9, 2939/10, 2941/7, 2965/6, 2968/8, 2969/5, 2970/10, 2971/11, 2976/10, 2978/9, 2999/8, 3002/10, 3003/11, 3009/10, 3012/10, 3013/9, 3020/9, 3021/10, 3288/10, 3290/11, 3296/3, 3298/9, 3317/12, 3395/10, 3492/10, 3590/9, 3591/10, 3592/12, 3683/10, 3708/10, 3738/10, 3739/10, 3740/10, 3741/8, 3784/9, 3791/10, 3816/13, 3829/9, 3865/12, 3933/10, 3954/12

Montreal, McGill Univ. Lib.
142: 2153/10
143: 1168/21*

Mostyn Hall 258, now New Haven, Yale Beinecke 661

Naples, Bibl. Nazionale
XIII.B.29: 1156/1, 1184/10, 1690/6, 1993/A5, 2602/2, 3156/4, 4019/79

New Haven, Yale, Beinecke Lib.
91: 138/1, 2183/1, 3165/1 **(9 in *IMEV*)**
163: 242.5/1, 1727/18, 2119/49, 2371/2, 2820/6, 3381/2, 3693/1
281: 2574/43
331 (olim Quaritch Cat.824): 4105.5/1
365 (olim Ipswich, Brome): 220/14, 576/6, 786/1, 799/1, 1367.9/1, 1767/1, 1823/4, 1870/3, 2064/2, 2673/2, 3190/13, 3256.3/1, 3372.6/1, 3694.3/3, 3736/3
593 (olim Phillipps 3338, Robinson Cat. 1950 item 28): 3653/3
661 (olim Mostyn Hall 258): 3928/24
Osborn a2 (= Osborn 5 in *SUP*): 778/5
Osborn a11 (= Osborn 32 in *SUP*): 1881/13
Osborn a13 (= Osborn 31 in *SUP*): 3428/71
Osborn fa1 (ex Laurence Witten, Cat.5 item 24): 2662/B8
Osborn fa2 (ex Laurence Witten, Cat.5 item 51): 1342/34, 1491/22, 2119/29, 2167/40, 4150/29
Osborn fa24: 2577/16 **(Osborn 22a in *SUP*)**, 2577/17 **(Osborn 22b in *SUP*)**

New York, Columbia Univ. Lib.
Plimpton 39: 2469/6
Plimpton 80: 1727/17
Plimpton 253: 4019/63
Plimpton 255: 1168/28
Plimpton 256: 1580.5/1, 3406/3
Plimpton 259: 326.8/1
Plimpton 263: 33/7
Plimpton 265: 2662/A31
Plimpton Addenda 2: 250.5/1, 324/12, 1971/2
Plimpton Addenda 3: 968/2
Plimpton Addenda 4: 2469/7

New York, Corning Museum of Glass
6: 28.8/1, 2192/3, 4154/9

New York, Glazier, see New York, Pierpont Morgan, series G

New York, Pierpont Morgan Lib.
B5: 430.5/7, 710/12
B11: 3581/2
B13: 3428/73
B17: 856.5/1, 3632/39
B21: 1328.3/1, 1408/4, 2627/15, 3079.8/2
G9: 1753/1, 2345/3, 3883/7
G39: 2300.3/1
M4: 1168/25*, 2825/7, 3787/9, 3928/27
M99: 1961/13
M124: 1168/26, 1173/7
M125 (olim Hastings, Ashby-de-la-Zouche, Quaritch): 2662/A25 = also 2662/A27
M126: 2662/A28
M249: 1913/25, 4019/53
M275: 746.5/9
M486: 2470/1
M690: 2662/A29
M722: 1439.8/1
M775: 674/11, 854/31, 935/18, 1009.5/1, 1224/2, 1929/6, 2766/3, 3757/2, 3955/21, 4230/9
M817: 3327/15
M818: 1459/A9, 2017.5/31, 3553/4, 4056/30
M875: 33/6, 399.5/10, 1426.6/9, 1637.6/10, 2361.5/10, 2736.2/10, 2831.4/10, 3218.3/10, 4189.5/9

M876: 70/1, 2516/19
M898: 1150.5/1, 1881/12
MA 717: 1933.5/5

New York, Public Lib.
Drexel Fragments 4180: 1/2, 664.3/1, 851.3/1, 1636.5/2, 2797.5/1
Drexel Fragments 4181: 3721.5/1
Drexel Fragments 4183: 3193.5/6, 3724.5/3
Drexel Fragments 4184, 4185: 3863.5/1
Drexel Fragments 4184: 2012.3/1
Drexel Fragments 4185: 1163.5/1, 1944.5/1
Spencer 19: 233/7, 263/7, 540/5, 1242/7, 1243/6, 1244/7, 1245/6, 1246/7, 1247/7, 1248/7, 1249/7, 1296/6, 1719/6, 2428/7

Northampton, Northants Record Office
Bru.I.v.101 (olim Brudenell): 2147/4

Norwich, Castle Museum
158.926 (4g–5) (olim St Peter Hungate Museum 48 158.926): 621.5/13, 879.5/13, 4110.5/13

Norwich, Norfolk Record Office
Case 17, shelf b, poem not found: 4128.8/1
Case 21, shelf f, no.68: 714/1

Nottingham, Univ. Lib.
Mellish Lm 1: 809/23, 824/49, 3632/36, 3637/1
Middleton Dc 7: 160/1
Middleton LM 7/1: 2872/15
Middleton LM 8: 2662/B5
Middleton LM 9: 245/37

Oslo & London, Schøyen Collection
194 (olim Penrose 12): 399.5/9, 746.5/8, 1426.6/8, 1637.6/9, 2361.5/9, 2736.2/9, 2831.4/9, 3218.3/9, 4189.5/8

Oxford, All Souls College
33: 710/5
39: 814/2, 841/2, 2686/A12, 2754/A2, 3352/2
103: 3491/2
121: 3422/3

Oxford, Balliol College
8: 2747/2, 3238/2
149: 14/1, 161.5/1, 427.5/1, 541.8/1, 830/1, 834/1, 847/1, 853.3/1, 1140/1, 1269.8/1, 1271/1, 1332/1, 1551/1, 1843.8/1, 1975/1, 2089/1, 2256/1, 3433/1, 3911.8/1, 4080/1
219: 3323.5/1
220: 733.5/1, 3902.5/1
227: 2145/3

228: 459/1, 4174/2
230: 0.3/1 (MS 320 in *IMEV*), 3478.5/1
239: 2167/11, 3273/11
316A: 1372/2, 1597/4, 1701/1
316B: 158.6/1, 1597/5, 1998/3
329: 935/4, 1168/32, 2766.3/1
354: 20/1, 22/2, 33.9/1, 37.5/3, 39.5/1, 65/1, 77/2, 103/1, 108.5/1, 112/2, 236/1, 294/1, 324/1, 343/1, 346/1, 354/2, 350/1, 374/2, 375/2, 418/1, 425/1, 465.5/3, 467/1, 470/1, 506/1, 548/1, 552.5/1, 597.5/3, 608/1, 675.5/1, 686/2, 687.5/1, 704/4, 717/2, 755/1, 769/1, 805/1, 825/1, 860.3/1, 878/1, 889/2, 890/2, 895/2, 898/1, 903/1, 914/1, 916/1, 977/2, 979/2, 1032/1, 1055/1, 1088.5/1, 1132/1, 1136.5/1, 1142.5/2, 1149.5/2, 1151/3, 1162.8/1, 1163/1, 1194.5/1, 1198/1, 1206.9/1, 1214.9/1, 1222/1, 1226/1, 1251.5/2, 1259/1, 1286/3, 1314/1, 1350/1, 1354.5/1, 1362/2, 1363/1, 1383/1, 1386/1, 1399/2, 1412/1, 1444/1, 1445.5/1, 1454/1, 1471/2, 1485/2, 1488/1, 1575/1, 1587.8/1, 1587/1, 1601/1, 1609/1, 1653/2, 1817/2, 1829.2/1, 1866/1, 1873/1, 1891/1, 1892/1, 1914/2, 1919/1, 1920/1, 1933.5/1, 1941/1, 1957/1, 2053/2, 2060/1, 2072.6/1, 2076/1, 2090/2, 2097/1, 2098/2, 2183.5/1, 2233/9, 2293.8/1, 2346/1, 2385/1, 2410/1, 2413/1, 2511/1, 2586/1, 2662/D3, 2678/1, 2681/1, 2732/1, 2771/1, 2784/1, 3074/2, 3087/4, 3161/1, 3171/2, 3187/A1, 3199.3/1, 3307/2, 3313/1, 3318/1, 3424/1, 3438.6/1, 3460/1, 3473/1, 3527/1, 3553.5/1, 3574/1, 3575/1, 3603/2, 3627/2, 3635/1, 3669/1, 3706.2/1, 3720/1, 3736/2, 3776/2, 3792.5/2, 3820/2, 3835/1, 3852/2, 3922/1, 3969/1, 3975/1, 3999/2, 4012/1, 4023/1, 4044.3/1, 4049.2/2, 4079.3/2, 4079.6/3, 4137/1, 4148/4, 4176.5/2, 4181/3, 4246/3, 4249/1, 4263.3/1

Oxford, Bodleian Lib.
Add.A.11 (SC 28746), wrong reference: 1777/1
Add.A.60 (SC 30161): 71/4a, 437/1a
Add.A.106 (SC 29003): 169/2, 1264/1, 1453/1, 1605/2, 2131/1
Add.A.268 (SC 29387): 256/1, 484/1, 1342/8, 2104/1, 2119/7, 2167/9, 3268/1 **(29837 in *IMEV*), 4150/7, 4287/1**
Add.A.369 (SC 29620): 654/1
Add.B.60 (SC 29179): 478/1, 824/9, 1706/1
Add.B.66 (SC 29273): 1672/1, 2073/1
Add.B.107 (SC 29560): 3270/2

(continued overleaf)

Oxford, Bodleian Lib.

Ashmole 191 (SC 6667): 2469/1
Ashmole 191 IV (SC 6668): 146/1,
688/4, 925/1, 2016/1, 2381/1, 2475/1,
3722/1
Ashmole 210 IX (SC 6795): 1436.3/1,
3848/4
Ashmole 337 (SC 6683): 365/b
Ashmole 343 IX (SC 6692): 562/2
Ashmole 349 I (SC 6704): 3087/1
Ashmole 360 VII (SC 6641): 1977/1,
3968/1
Ashmole 391 II (SC 6873): 688/1
Ashmole 691 II.5 (SC 6733): 3848/3
Ashmole 745 (SC 6953): 658/3
Ashmole 750 (SC 6621): 220/2, 906/2,
1781/2, 1939.5/1, 2119/33, 3117.2/1
Ashmole 751 (SC 8193): 1727/2,
2320/B5
Ashmole 759 (SC 6954): 410/1, 801/1,
1555.5/1, 2656/3, 2666/1, 3249/1,
3605/1, 3721/1, 4017/1
Ashmole 781 (SC 8113): 3943/2
Ashmole 970 (SC 6616): 120.2/1
Ashmole 1113 (SC 7391): 1422.5/1
Ashmole 1146 (SC 8212): 1151/2
Ashmole 1152 (SC 7861): 4215/1
Ashmole 1280 (SC 8216): 2736/1
Ashmole 1285 (SC 8221): 3200/1
Ashmole 1378 II,III (SC 7798):
412.5/1, 1199/1, 3771/1
Ashmole 1379 (SC 7683): 3525/1,
3754/3
Ashmole 1382 II (SC 7577): 4017/2
Ashmole 1386 (SC 8258): 365/c
Ashmole 1393 (SC 7589): 61/1, 63/1,
688/2, 2017/2
Ashmole 1394 XI.iii (SC 7596):
2656/4
Ashmole 1397 (SC 7760): 2627/2
Ashmole 1416 (SC 7611): 1823/1,
2656/5, 3721/2
Ashmole 1418 (SC 7613): 2656/6
Ashmole 1438 II,III (SC 7707):
2368/1, 3893/1
Ashmole 1441 (SC 7624): 1276/3,
2656/7, 2666/3, 3249/4, 3772/4
Ashmole 1442 (SC 7625): 410/2,
2354.5/1, 2656/8, 3754/2
Ashmole 1444 III (SC 7778): 3422/2
Ashmole 1445 (SC 7630): 407.6/1,
595/3, 1150.3/2, 1211.5/1, 1276/4,
1276/5, 3249/6, 3249/7, 3249/8, 3249/9,
3253/2, 3528/3, 3721/4, 3772/5
Ashmole 1448 (SC 7627): 3721/3,
3848/5
Ashmole 1450 VII (SC 7628): 2666/4,
3249/5, 3257/1
Ashmole 1451 (SC 8343): 1276/7,
3772/8

Ashmole 1464 (SC 7635): 3772/6
Ashmole 1477 II,III (SC 7719):
2627/1, 3422/1, 3848/6
Ashmole 1478 I,II (SC 7642): 2656/9,
3581.5/1
Ashmole 1479 (SC 7643): 595/4,
2826/1, 3581.5/2, 3721/5, 3772/7
Ashmole 1480 (SC 7644): 1276/6,
2656/10, 3928.5/1
Ashmole 1481 (SC 7722): 3848/7
Ashmole 1485 III.ii (SC 7652): 595/5,
3249/10, 3928.5/2
Ashmole 1486 (SC 7004): 1459/A3
Ashmole 1486 I (SC 7653): 2656/11,
3249/11
Ashmole 1486 III (SC 7009): 595/2
Ashmole 1487 II (SC 7654): 703.5/1,
801/2, 2666/5, 3257/3
Ashmole 1490 (SC 7010): 595/6,
1150.3/1, 1276/2, 2656/12, 3249/2,
3249/3, 3772/3
Ashmole 1491 (SC 7656): 1724/1
Ashmole 1492 (SC 7657): 3249/12
Ashmole 1524 VI (SC 8180): 980/1,
4160/4
Ashmole 11449 (SC 7554): 1441/1a
Ashmole Rolls 21 (SC 7081): 444/3
Ashmole Rolls 40 (SC 8447): 1364.5/3
Ashmole Rolls 52 (SC 7662): 1364.5/2
Auct.7.Q.21, number does not exist:
674/12
Auct.F.5.16 (SC 2581): 2752/1
Barlow 20 (SC 6420): 1913/4, 4019/19
Barlow 33 (SC 6488): 1727/1
Bodley 9 (SC 1851): 34.8/1, 1151/9,
3502/1, 4034.6/1
Bodley 26 (SC 1871): 29/1, 114/1,
525/1, 1260/1, 1437/1, 1606.8/1,
1871.8/1, 1964/1, 2231.8/1, 4207/1
Bodley 34 (SC 1883): 1871.5/1,
3570.5/1 **(SC 1898 in *IMEV*)**
Bodley 42 (SC 1846): 1940/1, 4088/1
Bodley 48 (SC 1885): 245/1, 824/2,
1992/1, 2233/2, 3632/2
Bodley 54 (SC 1975): 2320/B4
Bodley 57 (SC 2004): 3961/1
Bodley 61 (SC 2023): 1342/4, 2119/4,
2167/4, 3687/2, 4150/4
Bodley 75 (SC 2253): 2574/1
Bodley 85 (SC 2289): 3499/1
Bodley 89 (SC 1886): 1342/3, 1491/2,
1718/1, 2119/3, 2167/3, 4150/3
Bodley 99 (SC 1944): 3428/5
Bodley 100 (SC 1947): 1138/2
Bodley 110 (SC 1963): 2017.5/4,
2320/B3, 4056/3
Bodley 120 (SC 27643): 511/1, 766/1,
2574/7
Bodley 131 (SC 1999): 444/2

(continued overleaf)

Oxford, Bodleian Lib.

Bodley 175 (SC 27631): 716/1
Bodley 187 (SC 2090): 142/A3, 142/B4, 191/2, 400/3, 621/3, 798/3, 1003/4, 1141/3, 1204/3, 1223/3, 1490/3, 1822/2, 1935/3, 2001/B3 **(no number in *IMEV*),** 2077/2, 2329/3, 2340/3, 2729/2, 2832/2, 3133/2, 3254/3, 3273/2, 3275/2, 3281/3, 3282/3, 3287/2, 3408/2, 3518/3, 3649/2, 3716/2, 3863/4, 4035/2, 4134/2, 4151/3
Bodley 220 (SC 2103): 704/1, 4160/2
Bodley 221 (SC 27627): 124/3, 299/3, 1561/4, 2229/10, 2591/3, 3121/3, 3582/3, 4072/4
Bodley 263 (SC 2440): 1168/1
Bodley 264 (SC 2464): 4262/B1
Bodley 294 (SC 2449): 2662/B1
Bodley 315 (SC 2712): 1156/2, 1619/1, 4102/2, 4135.5/1
Bodley 332 (SC 2243): 400/4, 621/4, 1490/4, 2340/4, 3496/3, 3518/4
Bodley 343 (SC 2406): 3497/1
Bodley 393 (SC 2224): 317/1
Bodley 410 (SC 2305): 142/A4, 142/B5, 191/3, 495/2, 498/3, 565/3, 594/3, 798/4, 4156/3, 1003/5, 1127/3, 1141/4, 1150/3, 1223/4, 1321/2, 1822/3, 1935/4, 2001/A3, 2001/B4, 2002/3, 2058/3, 2077/3, 2114/3, 2283/3, 2298/3, 2329/4, 2596/2, 2729/3, 2775/3, 2832/3, 3081/3, 3133/3, 3147/3, 3254/4, 3273/3, 3275/3, 3281/4, 3282/4, 3287/3, 3339/3, 3350/3, 3408/3, 3649/3, 3716/3, 3802/3, 3863/5, 4035/3, 4134/3, 4143/3, 4151/4, 4239/3
Bodley 414 (SC 27880): 4019/2
Bodley 415 (SC 2313): 248/1, 778/1
Bodley 416 (SC 2315): 776/1, 1699/1, 2320/C1, 3851/1, 4047/1, 4129/1
Bodley 423 (SC 2322): 1039/1, 1083.5/1, 2347/1, 3429/2, 3687/3
Bodley 424 (SC 2324): 2268/1
Bodley 425 (SC 2325): 640/1, 1082/1, 1474/1, 1535/1, 1536/1, 3103/1, 4022/1, 4147/1
Bodley 446 (SC 2685): 245/2
Bodley 480 (SC 2020): 3706.6/1, 4138/1
Bodley 534 (SC 2252): 1247/1
Bodley 546 (SC 2285): 853.2/1
Bodley 549 (SC 2298): 784/1, 945/1, 1012/1, 1013/1, 1183/1, 1284/1, 1393/1, 1658/1, 1816/1, 1945/1, 2355/1, 2569/1, 2593/1
Bodley 565 (SC 2351): 475.5/1, 883/1
Bodley 596 (SC 2376): 561/1, 2574/2, 3612/1
Bodley 608 (SC 2059): 597.5/1
Bodley 622 (SC 2156): 91/1, 3280/1, 3970/1
Bodley 623 (SC 2157): 4181/1
Bodley 638 (SC 2078): 100/B1, 239/2, 370/1, 666/2, 803/1, 851/1, 991/1, 1306/1, 1388/1, 1507/2, 2251/1, 2756/1, 3361/1, 3412/3, 3444/2, 3661/1, 3670/2
Bodley 648 (SC 2291): 3444/3
Bodley 649 (SC 2293): 846/1, 1498.8/1, 1871.3/1, 3729/1
Bodley 652 (SC 2306): 4172/1
Bodley 686 (SC 2527): 199/1, 439/1, 447/1, 653/1, 824/3, 2233/3, 2590/1, 2592/1, 3632/3, 4019/17
Bodley 687 (SC 2501): 1003/6
Bodley 692 (SC 2508): 1013.5/1, 1798/1
Bodley 693 (SC 2875): 2662/A2
Bodley 758 (SC 2670): 1820/11
Bodley 770 (SC 2552): 233/1, 263/1, 540/1, 1242/1, 1243/1, 1244/1, 1245/1, 1246/1, 1248/1, 1249/1, 1296/1, 1719/1, 2428/1
Bodley 776 (SC 2559): 3928/4
Bodley 779 (SC 2567): 38/1, 82/2, 87/1, 104/1, 125/1, 126/2, 184/3, 201/3, 273/2, 276/1, 318/1, 443/2, 446/1, 483/2, 721/3, 733/1, 791/2, 794/1, 901/1, 902/1, 907/1, 1397/1, 1445/1, 1531/1, 1546/2, 1553/1, 1790/1, 1794/1, 1859/2, 1911/2, 2105/1, 2106/2, 2120/2, 2126/1, 2127/2, 2143/1, 2225/1, 2647/2, 2660/1, 2672/1, 2679/1, 2761/1, 2836/1, 2838/1, 2842/3, 2843/2, 2844/2, 2845/2, 2848/2, 2850/2, 2851/1, 2852/1, 2854/3, 2856/3, 2858/3, 2860/2, 2862/2, 2866/3, 2867/1, 2868/3, 2870/1, 2872/2, 2873/2, 2875/3, 2876/2, 2878/3, 2880/3, 2881/1, 2882/2, 2883/2, 2884/3, 2885/1, 2886/3, 2887/3, 2888/1, 2889/2, 2894/2, 2895/2, 2898/1, 2900/1, 2905/3, 2906/2, 2910/3, 2911/1, 2912/1, 2913/1, 2915/2, 2916/1, 2919/1, 2932/3, 2945/3, 2949/3, 2950/3, 2953/1, 2954/3, 2956/3, 2957/3, 2958/2, 2959/3, 2961/3, 2973/2, 2989/2, 2990/3, 2991/2, 2994/2, 3004/3, 3005/3, 3026/3, 3029/B1, 3030/1, 3033/3, 3035/2, 3036/3, 3037/2, 3041/3, 3042/2, 3046/2, 3048/3, 3049/1, 3050/2, 3051/2, 3055/2, 3059/2, 3060/2, 3063/3, 3064/2, 3067/3, 3068/3, 3091/1, 3202/1, 3380/1, 3383/1, 3384/2, 3386/1, 3388/2, 3389/2, 3452/2, 3494/1, 3624/1, 3655/1, 3664/2, 3814/1, 3855/1, 4173/1, 4176/1, 4266/2, 4267/1
Bodley 789 (SC 2643): 241/1, 1483/1, 1707/1, 1711/1, 2255/1
Bodley 791 (SC 2639): 158.3/1
Bodley 797 (SC 2649): 906/17
Bodley 814 (SC 2683): 1459/B2
Bodley 828 (SC 2695): 3561.5/1
Bodley 832 (SC 2538): 192/1
Bodley 840 (SC 27654): 1998/1

(continued overleaf)

Oxford, Bodleian Lib.

(continued overleaf)

Oxford, Bodleian Lib.

Holkham Misc.39: 3815.5/2, 3928.3/1, 3940/4
Holkham Misc.41: 3102/4
James 6 (SC 3843): 433/1b
James 34 (SC 3871): 3407/1a
James 43 (SC 3880): 71/1, 1989/1
Jones 8 (SC 8915): 2818.8/1b, 3430/1a
Junius 1 (SC 5113): 2305/1
Junius 56 (SC 5167*): 3428/9
Kent Charter 233: 1828/1
Lat.liturg.e.10 (SC 32942): 4181/2
Lat.liturg.e.17: 253/3, 1120.3/1, 1838.5/1, 3102/7, 3685/10, 3695.5/1, 4227.5/1
Lat.liturg.g.1 (SC 31379): 624/2
Lat.liturg.g.8 (olim Brough Hall): 1502/8
Lat.misc.b.17: 289/13, 4132/5
Lat.misc.c.66: 137/1, 461.5/1, 481/1, 556/1, 572/1, 735/1, 737/1, 768/1, 813.5/1, 855/1, 926/1, 931/3, 1187/1, 1270.8/1, 1331.5/1, 1344/1, 1386.5/1, 1727/13, 2217/1, 2231.3/1, 2263/1, 2281/1, 2597/1, 2682/1, 2760/1, 3079.4/1, 3443/5, 3793/6, 3943/5, 4057/1, 4148/13
Lat.misc.e.22(R) (SC 30586): 1502/1
Lat.misc.e.85: 349/1, 372/1, 561/8
Lat.th.d.1 (SC 29746): 65.5/1, 86.3/1, 593.5/1, 636.5/1, 672.5/1, 823.5/1, 849/1, 908.6/1, 1524.5/1, 1777/1 **(28746 in *SUP*)**, 1938.5/1, 2740/1, 3263.5/1, 3490.6/1, 3646.6/1, 3727.5/1, 3743.3/1, 3825.5/1, 4212.5/1, 4225.5/1
Lat.th.d.15: 824/46
Laud lat.95 (SC 1485): 465.3/1, 1840/1
Laud lat.114 (SC 649): 28.5/1
Laud misc.23 (SC 655): 403.5/1, 621.5/1, 879.5/1, 1297/1, 3985/1, 4110.5/1, 4160/1
Laud misc.77 (SC 997): 51/1
Laud misc.99 (SC 1123): 3327/F(i), 3786/1
Laud misc.104 (SC 1244): 1342/2, 2119/2, 2167/2, 3687/1, 4150/2
Laud misc.108 (SC 1486): 145/1, 166/1, 184/1, 201/1, 224/1, 351/1, 477/1, 496/1, 513/2, 721/1, 1114/1, 1550/1, 2839/1, 2842/1, 2850/1, 2854/1, 2856/1, 2858/1, 2866/1, 2868/1, 2871/1, 2873/1, 2875/1, 2878/1, 2880/1, 2883/1, 2884/1, 2886/1, 2887/1, 2890/1, 2894/1, 2896/1, 2897/1, 2899/1, 2905/1, 2910/1, 2915/1, 2918/1, 2932/1, 2945/1, 2949/1, 2950/1, 2954/1, 2956/1, 2957/1, 2958/1, 2959/1, 2961/1, 2990/1, 3004/1, 3005/1, 3017/1, 3026/1, 3029/A1, 3033/1, 3036/1, 3039/1, 3041/1, 3048/1, 3052/1, 3053/1, 3063/1, 3064/1, 3067/1, 3068/1, 3089/1, 3156/1, 3159/1, 3266/1, 3310/1, 3387/1, 3452/1, 3838/1, 4171/1
Laud misc.111 (SC 1550): 142/B3, 565/2, 594/2, 1003/3, 1127/2, 1150/2, 2001/A2, 2001/B2, 2002/2, 2058/2, 2114/2, 2283/2, 2298/2, 2320/B2, 2329/2, 2775/2, 3081/2, 3147/2, 3339/2, 3350/2, 3463/1, 3802/2, 3863/3, 4143/2, 4156/2, 4239/2
Laud misc.174 (SC 668): 3755/1
Laud misc.210 (SC 1292): 1356.3/1, 2017.5/2, 4056/1, 4073.5/1
Laud misc.213 (SC 1045): 142/A1, 142/B1, 191/1, 400/1, 495/1, 498/1, 565/1, 594/1, 621/1, 798/1, 1003/1, 1127/1, 1141/1, 1150/1, 1204/1, 1223/1, 1321/1, 1490/1, 1822/1, 1870/1, 1935/1, 2001/A1, 2001/B1, 2002/1, 2058/1, 2077/1, 2114/1, 2283/1, 2298/1, 2329/1, 2340/1, 2596/1, 2729/1, 2775/1, 2789/1, 2832/1, 3081/1, 3133/1, 3147/1, 3254/1, 3273/1, 3275/1, 3281/1, 3282/1, 3287/1, 3339/1, 3350/1, 3408/1, 3496/1, 3518/1, 3649/1, 3716/1, 3802/1, 3863/1, 4035/1, 4134/1, 4143/1, 4151/1, 4156/1, 4239/1
Laud misc.286 (SC 1151): 3576/1
Laud misc.330 (SC 819): 2504/1, 3102/1
Laud misc.413 (SC 970): 598/1, 2988/1
Laud misc.416 (SC 1479): 935/2, 1287/1, 1540/1, 2153/1, 3412/1, 3928/2, 3976/1
Laud misc.463 (SC 1596): 50/1, 56/1, 57/1, 58/1, 59/1, 82/1, 126/1, 184/2, 195/1, 201/2, 214/1, 273/1, 409/1, 443/1, 483/1, 539/1, 721/2, 728/1, 791/1, 1546/1, 1776/1, 1788/1, 1809/1, 1859/1, 1869/1, 1876/1, 1911/1, 2106/1, 2120/1, 2127/1, 2304/1, 2647/1, 2755/1, 2839/2, 2842/2, 2843/1, 2844/1, 2845/1, 2848/1, 2854/2, 2856/2, 2858/2, 2860/1, 2862/1, 2866/2, 2868/2, 2872/1, 2874/1, 2875/2, 2876/1, 2878/2, 2880/2, 2882/1, 2884/2, 2886/2, 2887/2, 2889/1, 2895/1, 2901/1, 2905/2, 2906/1, 2910/2, 2918/2, 2922/1, 2932/2, 2945/2, 2949/2, 2950/2, 2951/1, 2954/2, 2956/2, 2957/2, 2959/2, 2960/1, 2961/2, 2973/1, 2987/1, 2989/1, 2990/2, 2991/1, 2994/1, 3004/2, 3005/2, 3017/2, 3026/2, 3029/A2, 3033/2, 3035/1, 3036/2, 3037/1, 3041/2, 3042/1, 3046/1, 3048/2, 3050/1, 3051/1, 3052/2, 3055/1, 3059/1, 3060/1, 3063/2, 3064/11, 3066/1, 3067/2, 3068/2, 3266/2, 3384/1, 3388/1, 3389/1, 3664/1, 3766/1, 3767/1, 3813/1, 4266/1
Laud misc.471 (SC 1053): 2070/1

(continued overleaf)

Oxford, Bodleian Lib.

Rawl.C.86 (SC 11951): 71/2, 100/A2, 186/1, 401/2, 404/1, 444/4, 658/5, 824/7, 969/1, 977/1, 1447/2, 1460/2, 1511/1, 1841/1, 1907/2, 1916/1, 2179/1, 2233/6, 2464/2, 2584/1, 2625/3, 2719/1, 2737/2, 3113/1, 3203/1, 3503/1, 3531/1, 3612/2, 3632/8, 3798/2, 3847/1, 4019/68, 4019/76, 4020/1, 4082/1, 4090/1, 4137/2
Rawl.C.285 (SC 12143): 2017.5/7, 3561/1, 4056/6, 4172.5/1
Rawl.C.288 (SC 12146): 406/A1 **(12145 in *IMEV*)**, 621.5/2, 879.5/2, 1290/1, 4110.5/2
Rawl.C.301 (SC 12158): 105.5/1, 673/2, 1123.5/1, 4220/1
Rawl.C.307 (SC 12164): 704/3
Rawl.C.316 (SC 12172): 3632/9
Rawl.C.319 (SC 12175): 3428/14
Rawl.C.401 (SC 12255): 1342/7, 1491/4, 2119/6, 2167/7, 4150/6
Rawl.C.446 (SC 12297): 2516/3
Rawl.C.448 (SC 12299): 1168/4, 4174.3/1
Rawl.C.506 (SC 15353): 2903/1, 3609/1
Rawl.C.572 (SC 12417): 1730.5/1
Rawl.C.641 (SC 12487): 2668.5/1 **(Digby 53 in *SUP*)**
Rawl.C.655 (SC 15481): 1907/3
Rawl.C.662 (SC 12506): 1820/12
Rawl.C.670 (SC 12514): 142/A5, 142/B6, 191/4, 495/3, 498/4, 565/4, 594/4, 798/5, 1003/7, 1127/4, 1141/5, 1150/4, 1204/4, 1223/5, 1321/3, 1822/4, 1935/5, 2001/A4, 2001/B5, 2002/4, 2058/4, 2077/4, 2114/4, 2283/4, 2298/4, 2329/5, 2596/3, 2729/4, 2775/4, 2832/4, 3081/4, 3133/4, 3147/4, 3254/5, 3273/4, 3275/4, 3281/5, 3282/5, 3287/4, 3339/4, 3350/4, 3408/4, 3463/2, 3649/4, 3716/4, 3802/4, 3863/6, 4035/4, 4134/4, 4143/4, 4151/5, 4239/4
Rawl.C.699 (SC 12543): 3499/2
Rawl.C.813 (SC 12653): 79.5/1, 159.8/1, 172/2, 340.5/1, 366/1, 368/2, 430/1, 642.5/1, 649/1, 729/1, 733.1/1, 767/1, 813.3/1, 1017.5/1, 1180/1, 1253.5/1, 1328.7/1, 1329/1, 1349.5/1, 1450.5/1, 1768/1, 1841.5/1, 1926.5/1, 2228/1, 2245.1/1, 2261.8/1, 2271.6/1, 2409.5/1, 2421/1, 2439.5/1, 2482.5/1, 2496/1, 2498/1, 2500.5/1, 2529/1, 2532.5/1, 2532/1, 2547/1, 2552.5/1, 2560.5/1, 2757.3/1, 2821/1, 2822/1, 2827.5/1, 3098.3/1, 3228.5/1, 3713.5/1, 3785.5/1, 3804/1, 3903.5/1, 3917.8/1, 3962.5/1, 4020.3/1, 4190/1, 4210/1
Rawl.C.884 (SC 12718): 245/7
Rawl.C.890 (SC 12724): 245/8
Rawl.C.891 (SC 12725): 3428/15
Rawl.D.82 (SC 12900): 2662/D1, 4092/1
Rawl.D.328 (SC 15444): 34.8/3, 37.5/1, 271.5/1, 465.5/1, 644.5/1, 1137.5/1, 1142.5/1, 1162.7/1, 1173/1, 1297/8, 1354/2, 1634.5/1, 1793.9/1, 2233/8, 3087/3, 3292.5/1, 3318.8/1, 3372.5/1, 3444.5/1, 3892.5/1, 3922/2*, 3955/1, 4034.6/3, 4049.2/1, 4079.3/1, 4079.6/1, 4169/1, 4176.5/1
Rawl.D.893 (SC 13659): 836/1, 2356/1
Rawl.D.913 (SC 13679): 179/1, 194/1, 295.8/1, 1008/1, 1285/1, 1301.5/1, 1864.5/1, 1995/1 **(SC 14099 in *IMEV*, 'not identified' in *SUP*)**, 2037.5/2, 2229/6, 2288.5/1, 2516/22, 2535.5/1, 2622/1, 3361.3/1, 3428/16, 3898/1, 4256.8/1
Rawl.D.939 (SC 15409): 2794/1, 3479/1, 4258/1
Rawl.D.1046 (SC 13799): 2656/15
Rawl.D.1062 (SC 13814): 365/1, 734.8/1, 2384.3/1
Rawl.F.38 (SC 15563): 1459/B3A
Rawl.F.145 (SC 15432): 1093/1, 1105/C1
Rawl.G.18 (SC 14751): 4223/2
Rawl.G.22 (SC 14755): 2163/1
Rawl.G.59 (SC 14790): 3957/1
Rawl.K.38 (SC 15161): 403/1, 2198/1, 2457/1, 4120/1
Rawl.K.42 (SC 15165): 1552/1
Rawl.Q.b.4 (SC 16032): 220/5B, 3339.5/1
Rawl.liturg.d.5 (SC 15847): 4204/3*
Rawl.liturg.e.3 (SC 15799): 897/1, 1727/3
Rawl.liturg.e.7 (SC 15839): 3483/1
Rawl.liturg.e.41 (SC 15840): 4204/1*
Rawl.liturg.e.44 (SC 15841): 4204/2*
Rawl.liturg.f.36 (SC 15802): 1703/13
Rawl.liturg.g.2 (SC 15834): 779/1, 1708/1, 2119/35
Rawl.poet.f.10 (SC 14503): 2229/7
Rawl.poet.f.13 (SC 14506): 727/B8a
Rawl.poet.f.14 (SC 14507): 4132/1
Rawl.poet.f.32 (SC 14526): 34.8/2, 176/1, 461.8/1, 854/2, 1400/1, 1416/1, 1481/1, 1817/1, 1820/1, 1829.5/1, 2000.5/1, 2233/7, 2469/2, 3491/8, 3502/2, 3572/1, 3573/1, 3845/4, 3943/4, 3985/2, 3990/1, 4034.6/2, 4095/1
Rawl.poet.f.34 (SC 14528): 173/1, 227/1, 295.5/1, 456/1, 892/1, 1188/1, 1895/1, 2672/2
Rawl.poet.f.35 (SC 14529): 824/8, 854/3

Rawl.poet.f.36 (SC 14530): 333/1, 1334/1, 1446/1, 1510/1, 1652/1, 1982/1, 2437/1, 3065/2, 3832/1
Rawl.poet.f.118 (SC 14611): 6/1, 1762/1, 2052/2, 2323/1
Rawl.poet.f.121 (SC 14614): 595/7
Rawl.poet.f.137 (SC 14631): 1458/1
Rawl.poet.f.138 (SC 14632): 3428/17
Rawl.poet.f.139 (SC 14633): 3428/18
Rawl.poet.f.140 (SC 14634): 2574/6, 2742/14
Rawl.poet.f.141 (SC 14635): 4019/20
Rawl.poet.f.143 (SC 14637): 4064/1
Rawl.poet.f.144 (SC 14638): 2516/4
Rawl.poet.f.149 (SC 14641): 1913/6, 4019/21
Rawl.poet.f.151 (SC 14643): 1597/2
Rawl.poet.f.163 (SC 14655): 2031/1, 3327/4
Rawl.poet.f.168 (SC 14660): 2229/8
Rawl.poet.f.175 (SC 14667): 110/1, 170/1, 694/2, 771/1, 1375/1, 1718/3, 1781/5, 2021/1, 2080/1, 3028/1, 3187/C1, 3428/19
Rawl.poet.f.182 (SC 14674): 595/8
Rawl.poet.f.223 (SC 14714): 2516/5, 4019/22
Rawl.poet.f.225 (SC 14716): 201/5, 209/2, 213/B1, 574/1, 862/1, 1756/1, 1801/1, 1883/1, 2875/6, 2884/7, 2894/4, 2905/7, 2910/7, 2918/5, 2932/6, 2954/6, 2987/4, 3033/6, 3055/4, 3059/5, 3064/3, 3452/3, 3813/4, 3994/1, 3997/1, 4266/5
Rawl.poet.f.241 (SC 14732): 2320/A4
Rawlinson ?, not identified: 3449/1
Selden B.10 (SC 3356): 710/1, 809/2, 1294/1, 3661/2, 3798/1
Selden B.11 (SC 3357): 2662/A3
Selden B.14 (SC 3360): 4019/18
Selden B.24 (SC 3354): 100/A1, 482/1, 524/1, 564/1, 666/3, 679/1, 809/1, 913/1, 1215/1, 1507/3, 2043/1, 2221/1, 2242/1, 2461/1, 2478/1, 2820/1, 3327/3, 3361/2, 3412/4, 3542/1, 3627.5/1, 3660/1, 3727/1, 4284.3/1
Selden B.26 (SC 3340): 18/1, 21/1, 81/1, 93/1, 111/1, 353/1, 354/1, 385/1, 753/1, 795/1, 909/1, 1004/1, 1036/1, 1037.3/1, 1230/1, 1234/1, 1405.5/1, 1430/1, 1473/1, 1931/1, 2053/1, 2377/1, 2716/1, 2733/1, 3259/1, 3283/1, 3385/1, 3619/1, 3638/1, 3659/1, 3674/1, 3879/1, 4229/1
Selden supra 23 (SC 3411): 2320/A2
Selden supra 52 (SC 3440): 25/1, 26/1, 32/1, 40/1, 42/1, 45/1, 46/1, 47/1, 97/1, 284/1, 286/1, 289/1, 290/1, 291/1, 306/1, 314/1, 749/1, 944/1, 1464/1, 1641/1, 1642/1, 1643/1, 1646/1, 2908/1, 2909/1, 3015/1, 3288/1, 3289/1, 3290/1, 3298/1, 3299/1, 3317/1, 3534/1, 3544/1, 3816/1, 3954/1, 4117/1
Selden supra 53 (SC 3441): 124/2, 299/2, 704/2, 1561/3, 1867/1, 2229/3, 2591/2, 3121/2, 3582/2, 4072/3
Selden supra 56 (SC 3444): 3327/2
Selden supra 73 (SC 3461): 3848/1
Selden supra 74 (SC 3462): 2320/A3
Selden supra 90 (SC 3478): 688/3, 3848/2
Selden supra 102* (Ker Pastedowns 1744, Lewis & McIntosh MV84): 3428/93
Smith 27 (SC 15634), wrong reference: 433/1c
Tanner 17 (SC 9837): 82/5, 126/4, 273/3, 409/3, 443/4, 483/4, 578/2, 719/2, 791/5, 1546/4, 1809/3, 1859/5, 1911/5, 2105/2, 2120/4, 2304/3, 2647/4, 2755/3, 2839/5, 2843/5, 2844/5, 2850/5, 2854/6, 2860/4, 2866/6, 2868/5, 2872/4, 2874/4, 2880/6, 2884/6, 2889/5, 2895/4, 2905/6, 2910/6, 2912/3, 2949/6, 2950/6, 2951/4, 2960/3, 2989/5, 2990/6, 3004/6, 3026/6, 3035/5, 3037/5, 3042/5, 3048/6, 3051/5, 3052/5, 3066/4, 3067/6, 3068/6, 3384/13, 3389/5, 3664/4, 3766/3, 3767/3, 3813/3, 4266/4
Tanner 88 (SC 9914): 52/1, 3943/3
Tanner 110 (SC 9936): 2791/4, 3071/1, 3115/1
Tanner 169* (SC 9995): 3216.5/1
Tanner 196 (SC 10022): 961/2
Tanner 201 (SC 10027): 2500/1
Tanner 346 (SC 10173): 100/B3, 402/1, 666/5, 828/1, 851/3, 913/3, 1306/3, 1328.2/1, 1507/5, 2479/2, 2756/3, 3361/4, 3412/6, 3542/4, 3670/4
Tanner 347 (SC 10174): 530/2, 928/2, 1843/3, 2445/3, 3440/2
Tanner 383 (SC 10210): 3632/6
Tanner 407 (SC 10234): 35.5/1, 690/1, 832/1, 1278/1, 1560/1, 1870/2, 1927/1, 1929.5/1, 1961.5/1, 2065/1, 2380/1, 2472/1, 2507/1, 3087/2, 3119/1, 3207/1, 3443/1, 3456/1, 3522/1, 3524/1, 3666/1, 4035/8, 4129/2
Tanner 412 (SC 10239), wrong reference: 1823/5
Top.oxon.c.72 (SC 29764), wrong reference: 2167/42
Wood B.15 (SC 8586): 4258.6/2
Wood E.1 (SC 8505): 4258.6/1
Wood empt.18 (SC 8606): 1439.5/1, 3318/3
Wood empt.25 (SC 8613): 4182/1

Oxford, Brasenose College

9: 1728/1

Oxford, Christ Church
151: 1372/3, 1597/6, 1701/2
152: 1009.3/1, 1913/7, 2784/2, 3928/6, 4019/23, 4122/1
Allestree, unnumbered fragment: 3226/2

Oxford, Corpus Christi College
4: 3461.8/1
33: 4238/1
36: 2320/A6
59: 708/1, 1617/1, 2220/1
61: 530/3, 928/3, 2445/4, 2594/1, 3440/4
67: 2662/A6
132: 1286/4, 3373/1
155: 406/A3, 1026/1, 1342/10, 1374/1, 1491/6, 3507/1, 4150/9
172: 410/3, 595/9
198: 1913/8, 4019/24
201: 1459/B4
203: 809/5, 931/1, 3083/1
218: 400/5, 498/5, 621/5, 1490/5, 2340/5, 3275/5, 3282/6, 3496/4, 3518/5
226: 2656/16
237: 172/3, 233/2, 263/2, 540/2, 704/5, 981/2, 1163/2, 1242/2, 1243/2, 1244/2, 1245/2, 1246/2, 1247/2, 1248/2, 1249/2, 1296/2, 1488/2, 1719/2, 2335/1, 2428/2, 2574/8, 2590/2, 2714/1, 2987/5, 4125/1
242: 1168/5
255: 1346/1
261: 2347/2, 2364/1
274: 811/1, 2010/1, 2357/1
431: 127/1, 276/2, 2304/5, 2839/7, 2850/7, 2860/6, 2866/8, 2872/6, 2874/6, 2880/8, 2889/6, 2895/5, 2910/9, 2912/5, 2949/8, 2950/8, 2951/6, 2960/4, 3026/8, 3035/7, 3037/7, 3052/6, 3066/6, 3067/8, 3068/8, 3813/6, 4266/7

Oxford, Exeter College
47: 2000/1
129: 2516/7

Oxford, Jesus College
29: 66/1, 433/2, 695/1, 877/1, 1091/1, 1165/5, 1233/1, 1272/2, 1384/1, 1441/1, 1833/1, 1948/1, 2070/2, 2128.5/1, 2284.5/1, 2687/1, 3474/1, 3517/2, 3607/1, 3704/1, 3828/2, 3873/1, 3967/2, 4047/2, 4051/1, 4085/1, 4162/1
39: 3327/F(ii), 3786/2

Oxford, Lincoln College
Lat. D. 89, not identified: 2053/3
Lat.52: 400/6, 498/6, 621/6, 1150/5, 1204/5, 1490/6, 2298/5, 2329/6, 2340/6, 2775/5, 3081/5, 3339/5, 3463/3, 3496/5, 3518/6, 3863/7, 4143/5
Lat.100: 2232/1
Lat.129 (no number in *IMEV*): 1378.5/1, 3632/14
not identified: 4181/13

Oxford, Magdalen College
27: 1228/1, 3327.5/1
30: 3757/1
60: 420/1, 3640/1
72: 2320/B7
93: 541.8/2, 830/2, 834/2, 847/2, 1140/2, 1153/1, 1271/2, 1304/1, 1332/2, 1551/2, 1569/1, 1975/2, 2256/2, 2796/1, 3433/2
213: 2662/C3
Charter misc. 306: 941/1
St Peter-in-the-East 18.e: 1718/5

Oxford, Merton College
23.b.6 (Ker Pastedowns 919): 1979/8
68: 1357/1, 1950/1
120: 3398/1
204: 1727/4
248: 103.5/1, 759/1, 760/1, 797/1, 906/4 **(should be 4180)**, 1034.5/1, 1143/1, 1145/1, 1289/1, 1353/1, 1373/1, 1577/1, 1749/1, 1832/1, 2145/1, 2239/1, 2284.8/1, 2337/1, 2684/1, 2787/2, 2829/1, 3212/1, 3216/1, 3218/1, 3246.5/1, 3355/1, 3403/1, 3549/1, 3699/2, 3713/1, 3803/1, 4054/1, 4130/1, 4180/1 321: 2698/3, 4113/3

Oxford, New College
51: 3856/1
88: 1129/1, 1978/1, 2042/1, 3969/2
266: 2662/C4
310: 1703/5
314: 4019/25
319: 1597/7
320: 3228/1
326: 2662/A7

Oxford, Oriel College
79: 1459/B5, 1919/2

Oxford, Queen's College
161: 800/1
207: 1370/1, 2577/4
324: 3499/5
383: 1656/1
389: 406/A4

Oxford, St John's College
6: 2516/8, 2742/3
56: 1037.5/1, 2574/9, 3845/5, 4099/2, 4246/4
57: 1929/1, 2375/1, 3412/7, 3428/24, 3452.6/1
76: 3580/1
94: 2372/1
138: 3428/25
173: 3558/1

209: 3306/1
266 (256 in *IMEV*): 3928/28
Arch A **50**: 1721/9

Oxford, Trinity College

7: 2787/3
15: 3428/26
16A: 3428/27
16B: 1193/2
21: 1597/8
29: 2662/D2
38: 3748/1
49: 1151/4, 1913/9, 4019/3
57: 50/2, 56/2, 57/2, 58/2, 59/2, 82/6,
126/9, 184/5, 201/6, 273/4, 409/4,
443/6, 483/6, 578/3, 719/3, 721/5,
791/7, 1546/6, 1676/1, 1788/2, 1809/5,
1859/7, 1869/4, 1876/2, 1911/7, 2105/3,
2106/4, 2120/5, 2127/4, 2647/5, 2755/5,
2780/2, 2842/6, 2843/6, 2844/7, 2848/5,
2854/8, 2856/6, 2858/6, 2860/7, 2862/3,
2868/7, 2875/7, 2876/5, 2878/6, 2880/9,
2882/4, 2884/9, 2886/5, 2887/5, 2889/7,
2905/9, 2906/5, 2918/6, 2922/4, 2945/6,
2954/7, 2956/5, 2957/6, 2959/5, 2961/6,
2973/4, 2987/6, 2989/7, 2990/8, 2991/5,
2994/5, 3004/8, 3005/5, 3017/5,
3029/A3, 3033/7, 3036/6, 3041/6,
3042/6, 3046/5, 3048/8, 3050/4, 3051/6,
3055/5, 3060/5, 3063/6, 3266/3, 3388/6,
3389/7, 3664/5, 3766/4, 3767/4

Oxford, University College

33: 4083/1
45: 1458/2
60: 824/11
64: 301.5/2, 1397.5/2, 1664.5/2,
4076.5/2
78: 4204/4*
96: 3684/1
97: 2017.5/8, 4056/7
123: 1728/2
142: 1184/4, 3401/1, 3428/28
154: 3114/1, 4117/5, 4215/2, 4254.5/1,
4255/2
181: 233/3, 263/3, 540/3, 1242/3,
1243/3, 1244/3, 1245/3, 1246/3, 1247/3,
1248/3, 1249/3, 1296/3, 1719/3, 2428/3
188: 4132/3

Oxford, Wadham College

13: 2662/C5

Paris, Bibl. Mazarine

514: 197.8/10, 1367.5/11, 1727/20,
1736/2, 2017.5/29, 2270/11, 4056/28

Paris, Bibl. Ste Genevieve

3390: 197.8/11 **(339 in *IMEV*)**,
1367.5/12, 2017.5/30 **(no number in
IMEV)**, 2250/4, 2270/4, 4056/29 **(339 in
IMEV)**

Paris, Bibl. nationale

angl.39: 4019/51
angl.41: 1460/9
fr.1830: 1729/5
fr.7011: 2698/15, 4113/20
fr.12154: 310/A9, 313/A9, 814/10,
841/10, 2686/A9, 2754/A10, 3352/10
fr.13342: 2320/A14
fr.25458: 134/2, 158/2, 844/2, 922/3,
2176/2, 2567/2, 3162/2, 4014/2, 4256/2
lat.3638: 1502/15
n.a.lat.693: 993/1

Pavia, Univ. Lib.

69: 2704/2

Pearson of Cambridge Cat.13, 1953, item 219, now privately owned, was part of Beinecke Osborn fa.1:

2662/D10

Penrose

6, ? = Penrose 10, now Tokyo,
Takamiya 32
12, now Oslo/London, Schøyen 194

Peterborough, Cathedral Lib.

Fragments: 3271.5/1

Peterborough, Central Lib.

s.n.: 875/7, 882/3

Petworth House, Lord Leconfield

7: 1913/24, 4019/13
97: 595/23
99: 3249/30

Philadelphia, Free Lib.

Lewis 304: 935/19
Lewis 314: 1168/22*

Philadelphia, Rosenbach Foundation

439/16: 1168/30
1083/29: 2662/A32
1083/30: 1597/23, 2229/44
1084/1: 1913/27, 4019/55
1084/2: 4019/62

Philadelphia, Univ. of Pennsylvania

Eng.1: 3428/78, 3755/7, 3938/1
Eng.8: 3428/81
Lat.33: 704/14
Lat.35: 1270.2/4
Smith 4: 595/25, 2666/9, 2729.5/1,
2826/6, 3249/33

Phillipps 3338 Robinson Cat.1950 item 28, now New Haven, Yale, Beinecke 593

Phillipps (=8336), now British Lib. Add.46919

Phillipps 8820, now Tokyo, Takamiya 4

(continued overleaf)

EL 34.B.7: 2391/1, 2471/1, 2474/1, 2560/1, 2792.3/1, 3238/8
EL 34.B.60 (EL 1160 in *IMEV*): 1333/1, 2494/1
HM 1: 715/1
HM 2: 716/12
HM 55: 1805/1
HM 64: 970/8, 1905/5, 3453/8
HM 111: 407/1, 783/1, 930/1, 2221/3, 2222/1, 2229/41, 2428/6, 2538/1, 3082/1, 3224/1, 3402/1, 3407/1, 3480/1, 3788/2, 3831/1, 3854/2, 4066/1, 4234/1, 4251/2
HM 114: 1459/B17, 3327/16, 3553/5
HM 115: 2574/40
HM 124: 1342/35, 1491/23, 2119/30, 2167/41, 4150/30
HM 125: 3429/17
HM 126: 727/B13
HM 127: 465/1, 611/3, 1833.5/1, 2017.5/28, 3459/1, 4056/27
HM 128: 671/6, 1459/B18, 1583/7, 3429/18
HM 129: 25/13, 26/14, 27/1, 32/11, 40/8, 43/7, 45/11, 46/10, 47/11, 79/9, 89/9, 97/11, 132/8, 284/11, 286/11, 288/9, 289/14, 290/7, 291/10, 306/11, 314/12, 385/5, 416/7, 485/10, 1117/8, 1118/10, 1136/9, 1144/7, 1464/11, 1469/7, 1482/13, 1494/10, 1518/6, 1519/10, 1521/9, 1525/3, 1538/4, 1641/10, 1642/11, 1643/12, 1645/9, 1646/10, 1647/10, 1648/9, 1657/9, 1862/8, 1912/8, 2084/8, 2094/9, 2191/1, 2301/9, 2670/4, 2859/7, 2907/6, 2926/7, 2927/7, 2930/9, 2935/7, 2936/9, 2937/10, 2938/8, 2939/9, 2940/6, 2941/6, 2965/5, 2968/7, 2969/4, 2970/9, 2971/10, 2976/9, 2978/8, 2999/7, 3002/9, 3003/10, 3009/9, 3012/9, 3013/8, 3018/12, 3020/8, 3021/9, 3215/4, 3288/9, 3289/10, 3290/10, 3296/4, 3298/8, 3317/11, 3393/7, 3395/9, 3399/4, 3492/9, 3560/3, 3590/8, 3591/9, 3592/11, 3683/9, 3708/9, 3738/9, 3739/9, 3740/9, 3741/7, 3784/8, 3789/6, 3791/9, 3792/1, 3816/12, 3829/8, 3865/11, 3933/9, 3954/11, 4164/1, 4214/4
HM 130: 3428/83
HM 131 (olim Buccleuch, Quaritch Cat. 304): 979/12
HM 135: 1259/8, 2229/42
HM 137: 1459/C18
HM 139: 3428/84
HM 140: 401/8, 596/1, 720/1, 809/20, 1865/8, 2208/1, 2464/14, 3491/11, 3580/4, 3670/E, 3748/6, 3798/6, 3845/14, 4019/80
HM 142: 896/2, 914/11, 1045/3, 1370/6, 1721/8, 1727/16, 1748/3, 1761/11, 1831/2, 1961/12, 2118/5, 2119/48, 2306/2, 2352/4, 2469/5, 2473/2, 2577/14, 2711/3, 4200/8
HM 143: 1459/C19, 3327/17
HM 144: 658/12, 854/30, 986/2, 1629/1, 2574/41, 2714/13, 2784/15, 3121/7, 3437/7, 3504/6, 3955/20, 3985/12, 4019/75, 4215/3
HM 147: 1436.5/2, 2334/1
HM 183: 373/3, 824/44, 1261/2, 4112/8
HM 268: 1168/25
HM 501: 532/2
HM 503: 3098.5/1
HM 744: 666/10, 1221/1, 2326/1, 2389/1, 2640/1, 3102/5, 3150/1, 3777/1, 3853/1, 3889/1, 4122/3, 4160/9, 4233/1
HM 19916 (olim Davies-Cooke, Sotheby 15 June 1959, lot 205): 3815.3/1
HM 19999 (olim Dyson Perrins 33, Sotheby 29 Nov 1960, lot 109): 3708.5/1
HM 26054 (olim Helmingham Hall LJ II 8): 91/4
HM 30313 (olim Dyson Perrins, Sotheby Dec 1958, lot 42): 1364.5/7
HU 1051: 2026.5/2, 2751/1, 3571/5, 3887.5/1

Sankt Florian, Stiftsbibl.
XI 57: 4129/9

Saxby Psalter
Edwards Cat.624 item 247, now privately owned: 2119/31

Shrewsbury School
3: 662.5/1, 3428/63 **(no number in *IMEV*)**
6: 3870.5/1
Confessio Amantis fragment: 2662/D7

Shrewsbury, Shropshire Record Office (from Whitchurch Free Lib.)
3232/3, a land grant: 2160/1

Sotheby 10 Dec 1962, lot 145
A G Thomas, now privately owned: 1165/6

Sotheby 13 June 1983
olim Marquis of Bute, now privately owned: 2662/A23

Sotheby 15 June 1959, lot 205
olim Davies-Cooke, now San Marino, Huntington HM 19916

Sotheby 17 Dec 1952, lot 466
olim Meyerstein, now Princeton, Taylor Medieval 3

Sotheby 29 Nov 1960, lot 109
Dyson Perrins 33, now San Marino, Huntington HM 19999

Sotheby 9 Dec 1963, lot 120, now privately owned: 3585.5/2

Sotheby Dec 1958, lot 42, Dyson Perrins, now San Marino, Huntington HM 30313

Sotheby Feb 1959, olim Brudenell, now Austin, Texas 143

Sotheby Oct 1945, lot 1963, olim Harmsworth, now Geneva, Bodmer 110

Southampton, Central Lib.
SC15/97: 122/1 **(unnumbered in *IMEV*)**, 595/20 **(Town Lib. 3 in *IMEV*)**

Southwell, Cathedral Lib.
7: 462/9, 721/14, 2884/21, 2886/16, 2887/14, 2889/17, 2897/10, 2954/17, 3035/18, 4068.3/8

St Andrews, Univ. Lib.
DA775.A6.W9 (*IMEV* T T 66): 399/7, 1377/7
PR2065.A15 (no number in *IMEV*): 683/4
PR2065.R4 (no number in *IMEV*): 1979/7C

Stafford, Staffs Record Office
Bagot D1721/3/186 (olim Deritend House): 3529/1

Stanbrook Abbey
3: 1793.6/1, 4242.5/1

Steeple Ashton Vicarage
Horae: 914/5

Stockholm, Royal Lib.
X 90: 627.5/1, 1182/1, 1408/3, 2627/14

Stonyhurst College
23: 561/7
30 (A VI 23): 2167/35, 3687/13, 4150/26
43: 1752/2
64: 2577/11

Taunton, Somerset Record Office (from Bridgewater, Corporation Muniments 123)
D/B/bw 123: 17/1, 2377/3

Tokyo
Takamiya 4 (olim Phillipps 8820): 533/3, 2469/4, 4154/7
Takamiya 6 (olim Helmingham Hall LJ I 10): 550/1, 710/10, 933/2
Takamiya 22 (olim Sion College, Arc L 40 2/E 23): 4019/60
Takamiya 24 (olim Chatsworth): 439/8
Takamiya 32 (olim Penrose 6): 1451/1, 1724/5, 1913/26, 2052/8, 2662/D8, 3028/3, 4019/50, 4081/1
Takamiya 65 (Goldschmidt Cat.71, 1943, item 1): 2119/45, 3412.5/1

Trentham Hall, Duke of Sutherland, now British Lib. Add.59495

Trento Cathedral (in *IMEV* as Trienter)
88: 135.3/1

Uppingham School (archives, not yet found): 2627/12

Uppsala, Univ. Lib.
C.494: 3760.5/3

Urbana, Univ. of Illinois
71: 1342/39, 2119/54, 2167/46, 3687/19, 4150/34
83: 710/15
84: 1168/34
85: 2574/38

Ushaw, St Cuthbert's College
10: 2393/1
28: 1126/5, 1342/30, 1491/18 **(XVIII. D.7.8 in *IMEV*)**, 1815/6, 2119/26, 2167/34, 3685/9, 4150/25

Vatican
Borghese 298: 1179.5/1
Ottoboni 626: 2775/12, 3081/12, 3463/9, 4143/11

Washington, D.C., Folger Shakespeare Lib.
1186.2: 3559.8/2
1232.3: 2537/1
5031: 917/1, 1440/2, 3495/1
420312: 248/6, 778/6
SM.1: 2662/C10

Washington, D.C., Lib. of Congress
4: 1197.6/1

Washington, D.C., National Lib. of Medicine
4: 824/43, 2233/23, 3848/27, 4112/9
49: 970/9

Wellesley, Mass., Wellesley College
8: 3428/86 = also 3428/90 **(Sotheby 1922, lot 376)**

Wells, Cathedral Lib.
2 (no number in *IMEV*): 1687/2, 1739.5/1
Music MSS, Fayrfax Fragment: 3193.5/5, 3880.6/2 **(listed as lost Ely fragment)**

Wemyss Castle: 399/9, 1377/9

Westminster, Duke of (Eaton Hall)
Sotheby 11 July 1966, lot 233, then Quaritch, now privately owned: 1459/A10

Whitchurch, Shropshire, Free Lib., now Shrewsbury, Shropshire RO 3232/3, a land grant: 2160/1

Winchester College
4 (no number in *IMEV*): 1233/2
33: 127/3, 791/19, 1809/12, 1859/20, 1911/19, 2304/14, 2755/13, 2850/19, 2880/20, 2890/2, 2895/15, 2910/19, 2990/21, 3026/18, 3035/19, 3041/17, 3046/16, 3048/20, 3051/17, 3352.5/1, 3384/14, 3387/2, 3388/18, 3430.5/1, 3813/18, 3973/10, 4266/19

Windsor, Beaumont College
9: 3429/12

Windsor, St George's Chapel
E.I.I: 432/2, 1379/6, 1539/1, 1781/15, 3755/6

Wisbech Museum
21 (H.6.29 in *IMEV*): 2868/17

Witten, Laurence, New Haven
Cat.5 item 24, now New Haven, Yale, Osborn fa.1
Cat.5 item 51, now New Haven, Yale, Osborn fa.2

Wolfenbüttel, Herzoglichen Bibliothek
2819: 3115/2

Wollaton Hall, Quaritch Cat.1931 item 100, now Princeton, Taylor Medieval 2

Worcester, Cathedral Lib.
C.i.8, fragment (Ker Pastedowns 1984): 4265/4
F.10: 14/2, 89.5/1, 91.5/1, 427.5/2, 1628.5/1, 1848/1, 2300.6/1, 3101/1
F.12: 3909.2/1
F.19: 142/A9, 142/B13, 191/8, 400/11, 495/7, 498/12, 565/10, 594/9, 621/10, 798/9, 1003/13, 1127/9, 1141/10, 1204/12, 1223/10, 1321/7, 1490/10, 1822/10, 1935/11, 2001/A10, 2001/B10, 2002/10, 2058/9, 2077/8, 2114/10, 2283/8, 2298/11, 2329/13, 2340/10, 2596/8, 2729/8, 2775/11, 2832/8, 3081/11, 3133/9, 3147/8, 3254/10, 3273/10, 3275/10, 3281/9, 3282/11, 3287/11, 3350/9, 3408/11, 3496/9, 3518/10, 3649/7, 3716/8, 3802/10, 3863/13, 4035/7, 4134/7, 4143/10, 4151/10, 4156/7, 4239/8
F.64: 1142/1
F.126: 900/1
F.154: 906/15
F.172: 1703/17
F.174: 2684.5/1, 3074.3/1
Q.3: 142/B14, 498/13, 1003/14, 1204/13, 1321/8, 1935/12
Q.29: 4273.3/1
Q.46 (F.10 in *IMEV*): 1934/8
Q.50: 2288/1

Yates Thompson 57, now British Lib., Yates Thompson 13

York City Archives
House Book 6: 1186/1, 2214/1, 2215/1, 2216/1

York Minster
Abp.Thoresby's Register: 406/A11
Acta capitularia 1410–1429: 3820.5/1
Add.2 (no number in *IMEV*): 1734/1
XVI.K.6 (formerly XVI.G.5): 914/6, 1963/1, 1981/1, 2892/1, 4049.6/2
XVI.K.16: 2320/B15
XVI.L.12: 220/13, 406/B2
? XVI.M.4: 4204/10*
(not identified): 1621/2

York, North Yorks County Lib.

Yorks Philosophical Soc., York Plays (Scriveners'): 1273/2

INDEX OF PRINTED BOOKS

Mostly marginalia, insertions on flyleaves, fragments in bindings, etc.

Bristol, Clifton College
Norton's Ordinal (not a manuscript): 3249/27, 3772/20

Buckland House, now at Coughton Court
Mirror of Sinners (not sold at Christie's 20 Dec 1972): 3195/3

Cambridge, University Lib.
Res.b.162, now Ff.150.a.4: 3783.5/1

Kendal, Grammar School
de Clavasio, Summa de casibus conscientiae: 209/4

Kraus Sale Cat.93, Item 91: 627.8/1

Location unknown
Tractatus Sancti Bonaventure doctoris: 652/1

London, British Lib.
643.m.4, transcripts of Otho A.18 in Urry's Chaucer: 809/21
C.10.b.23, Caxton, Game of Chess: 1594/1
C.21.d.7, Caxton, Mirror of the world: 1409.1/1
C.40.m.9–11, Bagford Ballads: 1534/2
IA.3420, several tracts bound together; this poem is in fact at the end of IA.2856: 0.1/1
IB.49408, Caxton, Alliaco Meditationes: 324/11, 761/2, 4106/3
IB.49437, Caxton, Cordiale: 3818/3 **(IB.49408 in *IMEV*),** 4106.5/1
IB.55252, Trevisa, Bartholomaeus Anglicus: 3999/3, 4098.8/1

Manchester, Rylands Lib.
Pynson, Chaucer: 4123.5/1

New York, Pierpont Morgan Lib.
Acc.No.676 (673 in *IMEV*), Caxton, Dictes or Sayengis: 1602.5/1
Acc.No.698, Caxton, Royal Book: 1489.5/1, 2695.5/1, 3662.5/1, 3976.5/1
Acc.No.775, Boethius, De consolatione philosophiae: 2013/1
Acc.No.35083, Life of St Winifred: 2536.5/1
Acc.No.53095, Kynge, Great Herbal: 1409.5/1

Oxford, All Souls College
Capgrave, Commentary on the Creeds: 108/1

Oxford, Balliol College
695 h 6 (formerly 575.g.6), Lazius: 727/2

Oxford, Bodleian Lib.
80.G.40.Med: 2990/23, now with MS Eng.poet.e.94
Gough 173, Gough Horae, de Worde: 2749.5/1
Malone 941, Launfal fragments: 1184/3

Oxford, Corpus Christi College
Glanville, De proprietatibus rerum: 312.5/1, 1270.1/1

Ripon, Minster Lib.
Cicero's Epistles: 3571/3

Rosenbach Foundation
678, Boethius, De disciplina scholarum: 497/4, 2755.5/2

INDEX OF EPITAPHS AND INSCRIPTIONS

These are all epitaphs at parish churches unless otherwise stated. None has been verified.

INDEX OF UNIDENTIFIED, MISSING AND DESTROYED MANUSCRIPTS

Unless stated to have been destroyed, the items in this list are those I have failed to identify or find.

Stephens, Sir George

Stephens, Sir George, destroyed: 3327/E

Stockdale Hardy, Leicester Psalter: 2033/1

Temple, Newton Park, Sotheby June 16 1943, lot 153: 2516/23

Tenison: 704/17, 4160/11

Thompson, Portland Oregon (olim Amherst 20): 534/2, 1011/2, 2442/2, 2577/12, 2650.5/2, 2659.3/2, 2659.6/2

Tiverton Parish Church, on cover of a Primer, not found: 3580/3

Transcript made for Richard Boylston, 1712: 4252/1b

Transcript by Bradshaw: 3118.4/1b

Transcript by Bülbring: 3442/2a

Transcript by Langham Rokeby, 1815: 4252/1c

Transcript by Sir Thomas Rokeby, 1654: 4252/1a

Transcript by Stukeley: 3118.4/1a

Transcript by T Park: 260/1b

Tregaskis Sale Cat. 1919: 1168/24*

Uppingham School, not found, archives being re-organised: 2627/12

Wilton Corporation, not found: 3236/3

Witten, Laurence, New Haven, cat.5 item 47: 2033.5/1

Yates, W., Manchester, sold 1893, (by poet or scribe called Billyng): 427/1, 644/1, 704/13, 1703/11, 2742/12

York Minster: 1621/2, 4204/10*